TRUE **LEADERSHIP**
WHERE IS IT?

BIG **POLITICS** & BIG **BUSINESS**

Steve Lundquist

True Leadership leads for the benefit of all of us
and for each of us, not just for some of us.

WWW.TRUELEADERSHIP.ORG

Acknowledgments

I have just a few people I want to acknowledge in my drive to publish this book.

My wife, Kathy – for her patience and years of support, especially, my continuous talk of the big changes we need in our world.

The technical support people - who have guided the process of getting this book published.

Bill Greenleaf - my Editor – who became a personal friend

Amy Dennison and Elaine Meszaros – Website and Social Media Developer

Todd Vaske and Chris Peterson – Video Production

Rachel and James Anderson – Publicity and Print Production

Doug McDonald – Audio Book Production

Charles Hubbell – Audio Book Narrator

My Family and Friends for reading, discussion and critical support of the concepts within the book – Larry, Bob, Nancy, Jeanne, Bill, Lou, Sheri, and Julie.

Table of Contents

Introduction

Big Politics and Big Business Leadership

"A true leader has the confidence to stand alone, the courage to make tough decisions, and the compassion to listen to the needs of others. He does not set out to be a leader, but becomes one by the equality of his actions and the integrity of his intent."

– Douglas MacArthur

In this book, you'll see that I take some hard punches at Big Business leadership and Big Politics leadership. Yet, I have the utmost respect for these institutions. After all, they built our democracy into the institution other countries admire and want to emulate. And they've created the largest economy in the world, bringing many of us well into a middle class never before imagined.

However, over the years, I have become soured on the motivation of current top-level leaders of Big Business and Big Politics. Beginning thirty to forty years ago and accelerating over the last twenty years, decisions—and/or lack of decisions—by these two groups has led to several intolerable and life-threatening issues. We see division amongst citizens, stagnant wages, a decline of the middle class, a planet on the verge of collapse, and unnecessary taxpayer

1

cost from legislation that does not solve the problem, no matter what the problem.

In this book, I will discuss why we remain in this leadership debacle and how we can get out of it. I will include examples of leadership issues plaguing our country. Contrary to the belief of our former president Donald Trump, we in the U.S. cannot independently solve world issues, nor can we retreat from the world. As always, we must take the lead role in advocating, guiding, and supporting democracy and solutions to world problems.

With the technological and societal changes of the last fifty years, the world has become a one-body politic and a one-world economy. Today, every significant issue is global and affects all of us, not just some of us. The Coronavirus that swept through the world in early 2020 is the latest crisis to threaten a healthy human existence. However, pandemics and other predictable threats will continue to occur regularly until we demand from our leaders a solution to the root cause of the problem. Unfortunately, precious time is slipping away to implement the required world-saving solution.

We must demand a defining change to our highest level leadership in both Big Politics and Big Business to ensure an everlasting sustainable world. It is these two institutions that will have the most impact on the future of the world, and accordingly will require the most change.

When I refer to Big Politics, I'm talking about the federal political system.

Companies that I define as Big Business are businesses with annual revenue of over $10 billion or profit of over $1 billion.

Who is Steve Lundquist?

I have been in senior management for small businesses or small business consulting all my adult life. In all positions, I reported directly to the business president and was part of the leadership team. As a small business consultant from 1998 to 2006, I helped each client company president and leadership team grow the company or, in some cases, turn around their failing business. I have hired, managed, and mentored many people over my career. I am a general expert in accounting and tax, and I am familiar with business processes and tax processes of not only the U.S. but multiple other countries. I was significantly involved in three private equity transactions.

I led many people within each organization and interfaced with many more from all areas of the business: sales, production, engineering, information technology, marketing, service, accounting, and many others.

I'm also a student of history and current events, which is why, after forty years of observation, listening, and continuous ad hoc learning, I have come to some startling conclusions about the factors that collide in our relationships, friendships, leadership, business, politics, and the global issues of our world.

I have no Ivy League credentials, a Big Business CEO title, or a Senate or House member designation. Yet I believe, like you probably believe, that we are uniquely qualified to render observation and judgment of our current top-level leadership. Why? Because we are the people living with a lack of leadership in today's time of significant change and its catastrophic impact on our lives and lives all around us. However, you and I have a role in this leadership vacuum. We must become better at choosing our leaders and then helping them create the change required to cultivate a better life for all of us.

Let's begin this monumental task together.

Part I

Why Are Top-Level Big Politics and Big Business Leaders and Institutions Failing Us and the Planet?

Chapter 1

Critical Signs of Missing Top-Level Leadership

"One of the tests of leadership is the ability to recognize a problem before it becomes an emergency."

— Arnold Glasow

Factors that threaten a sustainable future for us and our planet

We are living in an era of unprecedented importance. Our lives, and the life of the planet, depend on our ability to change our human behavior. Just a few decades ago, our perception of a sustained future for us and the coming generations looked almost perfect. The Cold War ended. Cell phones seized the preferred communication device title. Personal computers made everything faster. The Internet was beginning to show some real promise. Television blossomed to hundreds of choices and channels. And federal budgets were balancing. Everything looked rosy.

But are we moving in the right direction?

I believe most of us could agree that the following are the simplest of goals for our sustainable future:

- A prosperous economy that provides us meaningful work and a reasonable paycheck.

- An education system that teaches our children well and prepares them for the future.

- A secure and safe place to live—which includes a healthy planet.

- A reasonable cost to live without passing some of that cost to our children.

- And Finally and Importantly, freedom from tyranny from any source.

Throughout human history, we have had good times and bad. In centuries past, good times were defined by lives without conflict and enough food and water to sustain us and a belief that we could defend ourselves from attacks by others. Bad times were a lack of food and water or conflict with neighboring peoples. . .or both. A battle ensued when leaders of one sect, tribe, or country attacked another, usually to increase their landholdings and capture resources and treasure. The loser of such conflict became subject to the leadership of the conqueror. Conflict also occurred when the leadership of a sect, tribe, or country was overthrown by its citizens, generally for bad leadership resulting in lack of food, higher taxes, ensuing poverty, or forced servitude.

In most of these conflicts, fear of an unsustainable future ignited the attack on either leadership or one's neighbors. Natural borders, water, mountains, rugged terrain, or expanded land holdings through previous conflicts always hindered or helped both attacker and defender. The sheer vastness of physical space helped or thwarted attackers and defenders alike, as did the latest weapons and human-made fortresses.

> For the first time in history, the threat of
> an unsustainable future lies in the balance
> for all of humanity.

Unlike in the past, natural borders, the latest weapons, and human-made fortresses are no match for today's issues. The planet has shrunk, and time moves so much faster than yesterday that we can no longer afford the luxury of procrastination. The threat of an unsustainable future has slowly crept into our perfect lives.

As evidence, the perfect sustained future vanished over the last twenty years. The attack on 9/11 took our feeling of security away. Russia infiltrated our election process. China is pounding on the doorsteps of our economic prowess. Our national politics have become totally partisan. Domestic terrorists are shooting up our cities. Big Business scandals of all kinds litter the news regularly. Our economy—and the world economy—collapsed under the weight of speculative investments. As predicted thirty years ago, our planet is heating up because we have done nothing significant to change the course of our behavior. Rogue nation-states are threatening us with newly developed nuclear bomb-delivery rockets. Finally, data security breaches are leaving many of us with concerns about what's next.

Two root causes are threatening an unsustainable future.

The first is a result of the success of our industrial and technological economic evolution. Fossil fuels have created a global warming crisis that threatens to strip the planet of its ability to provide our life-giving food and water. Information technology created a double-edged sword of an advanced state of knowledge and control while rendering perilously close to useless many of the barriers to attacks on our economic and security systems. The barriers are gone, and the world, whether we like it or not, is fully connected.

The second root cause of the fear of an unsustainable future is due to the highest levels of our political and business leadership and their apathy, unawareness, and/or misaligned leadership purpose. It is this root cause that we must eliminate forever. Only then will we be able to put behind us the fear of an unsustainable future.

Roller-coaster history of self-serving Big Business and Big Politics

Over the last 150 years, we have moved from the beginning of the Industrial Age to our current high technology age. We have had many ups and downs coming from self-serving strategies of Big Politics and Big Business.

We had the gilded age of the robber barons—or "captains of industry," depending on your point of view—in the late 1800s: J. P. Morgan—banking, railroads, steel, electricity and others; Andrew Carnegie—steel; John D. Rockefeller—oil; and Andrew W Mellon—multiple industries. These men amassed vast fortunes through their shrewd business dealings and the deplorable treatment of their employees—very little pay for backbreaking work and poor working conditions. During this period, Big Politics was controlled by Big Business through corruption.

From 1890 to 1920, the tide changed. Big Politics reined in some of the excesses of Big Business, giving workers better pay, better working conditions, and giving women the right to vote. Teddy Roosevelt and Woodrow Wilson supported legislation for better pay and working conditions. So did Henry Ford with his introduction of better line-worker pay. Ford said his workers must be able to buy his car. Wilson, although a staunch opponent of women's suffrage at first, eventually signed the legislation giving women the right to vote. After World War I, even though Wilson's League of Nations concept collapsed, his idea began pushing the world's democracies toward the vision for a united process for solving world problems. The United Nations was Wilson's concept.

Then came the Roaring Twenties, when Big Business again took charge, creating a substantially unsupported bubble in the relatively new stock market. The great market crash of October 24, 1929, started our deepest and longest economic depression. Many people lost everything.

In 1933, after four years of sliding further into an economic depression, Franklin Roosevelt pushed through his New Deal legislation, which brought several new concepts to the security of our country's citizens—Social Security and the Civilian Conservation Corps, to name just two. Even with the New Deal legislation, it still took until the beginning of World War II to fully recover from what began in 1929.

World War II brought much economic prosperity to the country with the building of needed war machinery. Women became a significant factor in the United States workforce, setting some of the ground rules for their vastly increased workforce participation over the '50s, '60s, and '70s.

After World War II, the country's economy and politics settled into a relatively stable pattern. There were ups and downs, but Big Business and Big Politics seemed to adopt the war philosophy that "We must work together to achieve our goals for the economy." Business colleges preached about five stakeholders:

- Customers
- Employees
- Stockholders
- Communities
- Suppliers

To be successful, a business must understand and balance the needs of all stakeholders. Accordingly, we had economic legislation during the '50s, '60s, and '70s promoting cooperation. Examples are pollution control with the creation of the Environmental Protection Agency and the breakup of AT&T to promote lower-cost phone service.

Then, in the late '70s and early '80s, economic philosophy went through another transformation. Milton Friedman's economic doctrine started questioning the premise that businesses had a responsibility to all five stakeholders. In fact, two stakeholders were added: executive team members and financiers (banks, brokerage firms, and private equity groups). Unfortunately, under this new economic philosophy, four of the original five stakeholders diminished in stature: customers, employees, suppliers, and the community. Only the executive team, financiers, and stockholders were left with any input on Big Business decision-making. Even worse, students started graduating from business schools with a mind-set that the only thing that mattered was increasing stockholder value, which pleased the remaining three stakeholders and left the rest of us out.

Leaders of Big Business quickly adopted this philosophy. It was much easier to lead for one purpose—increasing stock value—than multiple purposes.

In the mid- to late '70s, the formation of the Organization of Petroleum Exporting Countries (OPEC), the Middle East oil-producing countries' cartel, accelerated our economic philosophy change. The price of gasoline and other petroleum products skyrocketed.

We struggled to adjust to this new reality, but by 1980 our economy was poised to free fall. Ronald Reagan was elected in 1980, declaring that he could fix our economy. It took a while. We first had to endure recession and hyperinflation. Interest rates soared from 5% to 14% or more. However, by the next presidential election, the economy had recovered, and Reagan was re-elected.

All during the '80s, Big Business began embracing the new economic philosophy. Also, during the '80s, Big Politics started needing more money for campaigning. Cable television came into existence and pushed up the cost of election campaigns. Cable TV, with its continuous stock market coverage, forced Big Business to focus on short-term profits entirely. An unfortunate alliance between Big Business and Big Politics began to take shape.

This alignment accelerated when Newt Gingrich controlled the House of Representatives in the early to mid-'90s. Since Newt was

Republican and his political strategy aligned with the new business philosophy, the Big Business Big Politics partnership began to take hold. Big Money started flowing to the Republican Party. Since the Democrats couldn't be outside of this Big Money change in process, they had to adopt a similar partnership or run for office with significantly less campaign funding.

The country has now reverted to the robber baron/captains of industry era where Big Business and Big Politics are fully aligned. Legislation against Big Business interests has slowed over the last forty years to a point where most of us would say it's now nonexistent.

Now let's tie history to the missing leadership dilemma.

Our current Big Business and Big Politics condition is eerily similar to the historical alignment of the late 1800s. The tycoons of the 1800s would do whatever it took to make more money for themselves. They bought politicians and/or the political process with bribes and covert payments. Today's Big Business funds the lion share of campaigns for our highest political offices in the form of political action committee funding from companies, senior business executives, and substantial unknown other sources.

Global threats to Futuristic Sustainability

Because our world has become globalized in every way, disasters lurk around every corner. We have seen several major crises over the last twenty years, all of which had global implications. They have come in many different forms, which makes planning and solutions mind-boggling.

1. Global warming. Time is running out for our future and our planet's future. We're already experiencing deaths, destroyed lives, and the repair and replacement cost of global environmental disasters. I'll talk more about this serious problem in later chapters and in Appendix 1.

2. Terrorists inciting anarchy and bloodshed at home and around the world.

3. China's rise in the global economy and power spurred on by the complacency of Big Business and world governments in curbing technical and other pirating efforts.

4. Russia's reemergence into Cold War politics and tactics.

5. The continuing nuclear threat posed by small, non-democratic nation-states.

6. The rise in state- and crime-sponsored data attacks with the power to instantly cripple the world economy and democracy.

7. The monetary disparity between classes to the point of a virtual financial aristocracy holding power to choose leaders and laws.

8. The virtual collapse of the free-world economy due to the greed of a few bad corporate actors.

9. Bad actors heading up global businesses creating financial loss, undermining institutional trust, and causing death.

10. An undermining of the virtue of diversity and inclusion and the concept itself of democracy here and around the world by so-called world leaders who are promoting clannish separating behavior for their political gains and benefits.

These crises have impacted all of us with higher costs for products, services, and taxes. Many of us have been indirectly affected by the anxiety and turmoil surrounding these crises. The advent of accelerated change and rapid globalization make these threats even more serious than in the past.

Any of the above recent disasters can and will repeat on a scale so massive it will undermine our human existence in ways never before seen. Our national political and business leaders have been watching their effects but have done nothing to solve them. Big Politics attacks the other side of the aisle for their proposed solution strategies, accomplishing nothing, often reversing legislation enacted by the other party when they get control. Big Business thinks these issues have nothing to do with them unless it affects their bottom line.

The saving solution strategy must first acknowledge that these problems are related by their cataclysmic impact on all of us. The solution requires a new leadership model that connects our Big Politics and Big Business in a form that benefits each of us and all of us, not just some of us.

The 2020 Coronavirus pandemic

Let's examine the 2020 Coronavirus pandemic as a recent cataclysmic disaster and the failure of top-level leadership of Big Politics and Big Business.

Once we realized how serious this threat was to the U.S. and the world, several things became clear:

- The first response was a lot of finger-pointing about why we were unprepared for the pandemic and wasted time mitigating the dire outcomes.

- The federal government was unprepared to handle such a crisis.

- Big Business accepted no responsibility for anything to do with fighting the attacking virus—a lack of resources to provide needed supplies, drugs, facilities, and required staff to fight the virus.

- Partisan politics got in the way of implementing a non-partisan pre-authorized crisis economic plan.

Besides the elderly, most of the deaths occurred in poor communities of color. Most of the financial problems harmed, just like in 2008, our poor and barely above-middle-class populations, including financial and food security and record-breaking food shelf use. Most of the lack of supplies occurred because we had not discussed, let alone decided upon, what products are security products that must be produced here, not someplace else where another government or supplier has control over the distribution.

All of the pandemic's resulting trauma reflects the lack of connection between almost everything required to manage this type of crisis. This lack of connection originated from our own lack of solutions to our everyday issues and our lack of understanding of the trades we have made over the past few decades between security and profit.

The bottom line: our top-level leadership needs to move away from reactive thinking to futuristic thinking if we are to combat these crises. Plans and combatting strategies must be ready to implement immediately—hours and days, not weeks and months.

Covid-19 is another significant problem not well managed by our federal government and Big Business and another blow to We the People's safety, security, and well-being.

Which crisis will be next?

Can we afford to have our top-level leadership continue to be unprepared for these inevitable crises...or worse, be complicit in their occurrence? Blind ignorance, divisive politics, an attitude of "it's not my problem," and/or an unwillingness to tackle today's hard problems create a lack of proactive strategies for combating or eliminating their risk to us.

Chapter 2

Today's Top-Level Leaders Go Missing When Needed Most

"We cannot solve a crisis without treating it as a crisis. And if solutions within the system are so impossible to find, then maybe we should change the system itself."

– Greta Thunberg

We the People

For purposes of this discussion, I'm going to divide the citizens of our country into three groups, approximating one-third of the whole of us into each group.

The first group is generally Republican and wants a life as they know it without change or revert to the way things were. This is a mixed group. Many are older and white. Many have been displaced from their earlier life circumstance. Significant numbers live in rural America. Many connect well with the captains of industry in the loosest sense because they adamantly believe in their freedom to do as they wish. And finally, many are Evangelical Christians.

The second group is Democratic and is generally defined as

progressive, wanting continuous change for the better, to ultimately achieve the Great Society. "We're all in this together." Many of those in this group are younger, with much of their life ahead of them. Many are urban and suburban white people of all ages with incomes that run the spectrum. Many are people of color or varying ethnicity or disenfranchised people. Bernie Sanders and his progressive agenda have solidified much of this group of voters over the last few decades. Still, the entire group is much broader and will vote, in general, for the Democratic Party candidate.

The last group is in the middle—wanting life to improve but with as little disruption to their current life as possible. This group floats between Republican and Democrat. In actuality, this group is smaller, by a little, than the other two. Their demographics are closer to the Democrats but include many who would fit well into the Republican Party. Their voting is determined by the candidates that walk this line between change and no change and involves factors which depend on each individual's life priorities and circumstances and their belief in the candidate's ability to achieve their commitments.

All of the above is evidenced by the almost 50-50 split in federal politics, especially the presidency.

It seems unlikely that the voting electorate's two outer edges will change their voting preference under any circumstance. Therefore, evolving Big Politics to significantly and permanently solve our world's looming cataclysmic disasters requires a new type of politician or courageous existing politician. He/she must speak truth to all of us but must convince a significant majority of the centrist voters that major political change is required to save us and our world.

This block of voters must believe that their lives and the lives of future generations hang in the balance between life and death. These change-agent voters from the middle of the electorate of this desperately required political movement must permanently accept this conviction as theirs to foster and protect. We can no longer swing between political parties every election—which is one reason why, in Chapter 9, I'll be suggesting that it's time to eliminate political parties.

Still, we must elect politicians who know they are responsible for *all* of our lives and commit to the required long-term solutions that guarantee Futuristic Sustainability.

The true meaning of words from our country's sacred documents

The second paragraph of the Declaration of Independence states:

> We hold these truths to be self-evident, that all men are created equal, that they are endowed by their Creator with certain unalienable rights, that among these are life, liberty, and the pursuit of happiness. That to secure these rights, governments are instituted among men, deriving their just powers from the consent of the governed.

These words are backed up by the Preamble to the Constitution:

> We the people of the United States, in order to form a more perfect union, establish justice, insure domestic tranquility, provide for the common defense, promote the general welfare, and secure the blessing of liberty to ourselves and our posterity, do ordain and establish this Constitution of the United States of America.

Another document that we learned as children references our connection to each other—the Pledge of Allegiance:

> I pledge allegiance to the flag of the United States of America and to the Republic for which it stands, one nation under God, indivisible, with liberty and justice for all.

Our founding fathers wanted these sacred words to define the fundamental principles for the founding of our country. In these words was their hope that we would not discard the rights of the many, favoring the few or abandon the rights of the few in favor of the many.

And yet, I believe that this line between the few and the many is not a separating line but a connecting line. For democracy to succeed, this connection is its cornerstone. Throughout our country's history, it has been our citizen responsibility, as the governed, to choose leaders who will adjust to the times and propose and pass legislation that connects each of us to all of us.

> After almost 250 years, there are still many of us whose American Dream of life, liberty, and the pursuit of happiness lies in the hands of leaders who still believe the American Dream is only for some of us, not all of us.

We have fought wars over these words from our founding documents, both here and abroad. We have ended slavery. We have given the right to vote to half of our population previously denied such a sacred right. We have demanded that all citizens have the right to vote without exception regardless of color or state or local interference. And the list goes on.

Yet, after almost 250 years, there are still many of us whose American Dream of life, liberty, and the pursuit of happiness lies in the hands of leaders who still believe the American Dream is only for some of us, not all of us.

The Preamble to the Constitution begins with these three words: "We the People," big and bold. Yet our democracy has been hijacked in the last several decades by something that is not a "people." Big Business and its benefactors have provided so much campaign financing that all politicians are now beholden to them, not to We the People.

Recently I have heard individuals, even elected officials, misusing the word "liberty" when talking about the principles set forth in the above documents. These people refer to individual liberty as though there is an accepted separation of themselves or someone from the rest of us.

We clearly see, from each of our two founding documents and the Pledge of Allegiance, the direct reference to all of us sharing the same rights as each other, no more and no less.

It's time We the People solve this age-old problem once and for all or face the tragedy of extinction. We must understand the role leadership plays in the significant issues of the lives of all of us and each of us. We are not separate but inseparable. Therefore, that which *I* get automatically accrues to *we*, and that which *we* get automatically accrues to *I*. *We* and *I* are connected, inseparable, and anything less than this connection is not yet *us* or what we are striving to become in our businesses, our country, and our world.

Let me zero in on what I mean by the forgoing paragraph by putting it in the context of serious detrimental local issues. I will use two continuing real problems occurring in two very different sectors of our country: urban America and rural America.

First let's look at urban America. From the 1980s to today, heavy industry shed millions of high-paying jobs in urban America. Computer technology in the form of CAD/CAM (computer aided design and computer aided manufacturing) required fewer and fewer actual workers, leaving many cities decimated. Many workers of color, often the lowest paid, least skilled (generally the norm by design), and lowest in seniority, were first to go. These decimated cities with declining tax revenue charted a downward spiral into more and more desperation and crime.

Now let's see what's been happening in rural America. Over the last two and a half decades, smaller industry—usually serving larger industry—has left rural America in droves. Jobs left for China and other countries, and many of what remained were taken over by machines.

Clear hindsight shows we traded lower prices for lost jobs with no plan for how to go forward for either urban or rural America. Both situations occurred in many states across the country and are continuing in the same operating mode today...no plan for federal help, and certainly no Big Business help. Local governments in the form of states and cities do not have the financial power or the coordinated efforts to solve these situations as they come up.

Communities like these need jobs, not handouts. Both Big Politics and Big Business need to be leading from the future to create new jobs to replace those no longer needed. It can be done, but only from a connected world process. Decimated communities of color and decimated white communities with similar needs litter the landscape of our country. Why can't we see this? Silos of Big Politics and Big Business operating for their benefit (reelection or profit) will no longer solve today's problems. *We* are *I*, and *I* am we. We can force them to help.

Leaders go missing when we need them most

Our political leaders' focus changes to self-preservation or self-interest when solutions are complicated, especially when the political strategies for solutions are at opposite ends of the political left/right continuum.

In the case of businesses, when potential solutions favoring customers, employees, or the community are costly or seem contrary to their current business strategy, business leaders tend to avoid fights with their stockholders and their self-interest. It's much easier and more secure for them to engage politicians and the public with money and propaganda that favors the defeat of costly regulation.

In the previous chapter, we discussed the major problems threatening our democracy and the democracies of the world, and our largest global businesses. As outlined, none of these are easily solved. From the politician's viewpoint, political problem solutions rely on staying in office, which requires lots of money. From the Big Business leader's view, business problems require continued profitability and increases in stock price.

Therefore, the easiest way for both politics and business to solve related issues is to fund reelection campaigns in exchange for political favors, low-cost profitability increases for business, and reelection for the politicians.

We, all of us, are letting our top-level leaders get away with this power and greed exchange rather than finding real solutions. Businesses and We the People require capital to operate and live. When the largest financial institutions obstruct regulatory legislation to make more money, the economy can fall off a cliff, as it did in 1929 and 2008.

We, through Big Politics, must take action to make sure this never happens again. Unfortunately, Big Politics is not always on our side. Legislation enacted after the 2008 recession has been diluted to the point where it may be too weak to prevent a similar economic meltdown. Money for favors often gets in the way of hope of a better life for We the People.

> We can no longer allow the stock market to dictate our future.

Additionally, a sacred cow of our economic system of the last 100 years adds fear to our economy. What I'm talking about is the stock market. Whenever there is any significant crisis in any sector of our economy, this sacred cow freaks out and drops significantly. A sudden market fall scares everyone because it's how we all measure the stability of our economy. If its value drops dramatically for any significant time frame—even for just a few months—jobs are lost, homes are lost, retirement and savings are lost, and many of us living on the edge are scrambling to stay alive.

We can no longer allow the stock market to dictate our future. Big Business and Big Politics leaders are giving it power over the U.S. and the world economy because they are ducking their responsibility to each of us and all of us.

In later chapters, I will discuss much more about this phenomenon and why it impacts us, and how we can tweak the dial and significantly change its impact on our economic system and our future lives.

Special interests and unethical leaders use fear-based separation tactics

Let's be clear about who has replaced us as We the People. They are the groups that draw the majority interest of our legislators. We call them "special interests," and they are not We the People.

The most significant special interest is Big Business. With all its cash, Big Business gets much more legislative attention and beneficial action than We the People. This is also true of religious organizations, gun lobbies, etc. Yes, we know these special interests are groups of people seeking favor from our government. But we also know they are not all of us or each of us. They are *some* of us seeking favor from our government, often detrimental to the rest of us.

Whenever we choose to separate ourselves from each other, our life circumstances decline, and in today's world, our democracies decline. There are multiple symptomatic examples: war, discrimination, policing. But almost all stem from group separation: race, religion, ethnicity, sex, origin, etc. As we all know, all of these have created a life-and-death separation that, unfortunately, continues today. Some of us have privileges; others do not. In the extreme, some of us have life, others do not...and eventually, the rest of us do not.

We see this widespread attack once again on the democracies of the world—attacks by misguided or unscrupulous leaders whose goal is power and control. To retain or gain power, they need only to create fear in many of us, which then enhances the control of the "some of us" group they are leading. As we have seen time and again, fear is easy to create.

Political leaders of this type use other groups as the scapegoat for the problems they can't solve. They blame Blacks, Hispanics, Jews,

Muslims, teachers, the LGBTQ community, single parents, women, welfare recipients, other countries, other races, and the list is endless. Fear and control work in the short term but have proven to be the wrong solution over time. In the meantime, we all suffer until we realize we have been duped once more by a misguided or unscrupulous leader and must begin the long haul to take back our control and power.

But in today's fast-paced world, without a substantial mind-set change away from fear-scapegoating leaders, we may be doomed by problems not solvable in the remaining time frame.

> Why do we accept the lies perpetrated by leaders who use the fear-scapegoat strategy?

The fear-scapegoat strategy is easy to spot, and it would be ineffective if we did not react to it. So the question must be asked: Why do we accept the lies perpetrated by leaders who use the fear-scapegoat strategy?

First off, there is almost always a small shred of truth to the statements they make. Secondly, several individual personal factors can contribute to our erroneous beliefs. Finally, we humans tend to accept rhetoric from top-level leadership as truth, hardwired into our brains from childhood. "My parents would not lie to me. Neither would my boss, the president, my pastor/imam/rabbi, or teacher—any significant authority figure in my life."

As a historical side note, Adolf Hitler, a master of the fear-scapegoat strategy, never garnered more than 40% of Germany's voting public. Yet, he was able to control Germany for over a decade and exterminate the Jewish population—his scapegoat population—with the tacit approval of the German people. Many democratic governments are currently seeking to retreat into a similar so-called nation-state, closing borders, cutting off trade, separating from alliances, and canceling agreements. Interestingly, many of these things have eventually led to wars, the most costly enterprise in both lives and money.

Non-political leaders use the fear-scapegoat strategy too—our businesses, our religions, and any organization that seeks favored treatment from the rest of us.

Big Business uses the fear-scapegoat strategy to garner favored arrangements from legislators in the form of tax relief, government subsidies, mitigation of regulatory controls, avoidance of future costs, and the list goes on forever. They flaunt adverse outcomes: rising prices, loss of jobs, scared investors, loss of profits, threats to relocate, go broke, and any other negative statement about their business to garner the most favorable treatment by our governments.

Guess who pays the bill later on? We do. Need I say any more than the last recession?

Religions promote favored status through legislation for their views on morality for each of us and all of us. They are also good at demonizing people born with a mind and/or body that doesn't match their view. Again, this doesn't just create turmoil between all of us and each of us; it creates unnecessary costs and, most importantly, separation.

Other organizations use the fear-scapegoat strategy to pit groups against each other, creating decision gridlock and much higher cost in lives and money. For example, the gun lobby supports the minimum amount of gun control it can get Congress to accept, yet more people die in gun violence in the United States each year than most of the world combined.

Why do we do this to each other?

We should have learned by now that this type of leadership is not leadership. Any democracy, Big Business, Big Religion, or Big Organization promoting a fear-scapegoat strategy is misguided at best and, at worst, out to limit the rest of our lives in favor of the lives of some protected group.

Top-level leadership that pits some of us against others of us is not leadership

In U.S. politics, the relevant "less than all of us" groups are the Republican Party and the Democratic Party. The proper "all of us" group is "We the people of the United States of America."

Both parties are moving further and further from each other, and in doing so, they're turning us into adversaries.

Republicans believe everyone creates their opportunity and should solve their problems within the parameters with which they live, including those that they created themselves and those that we created for them—an individualism and/or tribalism conviction. Democrats believe all of us should have the same rights and opportunities and would create a society that promotes this belief, a "we're all in this together" conviction.

Both parties believe that the country's safety and security is the responsibility of the federal government. But Republicans believe "safety and security" refer only to physical safety and security: housing, food, etc. Democrats believe "safety and security" should include factors such as health care, education, and job security.

There are philosophical differences, to be sure. Still, instead of allowing those differences to define us, True Leaders in Big Politics should be looking for ways to bring us together despite our differences. Instead, many in leadership roles seem to believe that their best chance to hold their power is to keep us separated and pitted against one another.

How Big Business is failing all of us and each of us

What keeps Big Business from acting in the best interest of their customers, employees, community, and suppliers in addition to their stockholders...in effect, in the best interest of all of us and each of us, instead of just a few of us?

- Their missing connections between similar and dis-similar businesses.

- Their lost links to the broader marketplace.

- Their lost connections to a more comprehensive strategy and scope of opportunity.

- Their missing regards to We the People in a much broader way.

- Their missing links to a broader funding mechanism.

- Their ties to the existing limited stock market/stock price operating system.

- For many but not all, their ties to the luxury or for-profit only based economic system that rewards significantly when it works and can easily fall on its face when disaster hits.

- The herd mentality.

Let's talk about that last one for a moment. Here's how the herd mentality is reflected in the words of those who fall for it:

"This is the way it's been and the way it should stay."

"It works for me."

Then there's the favorite of those opposing change:

"That will never work."

I've heard that one many times over my business career of four decades. I'd ask, "Why not? Have you tried it?"

Often I received a shrug and shake of the head.

"Then how do you know it won't work?" I'd say. "Let's try it."

We must attempt change and reevaluate the outcome, adjust for the issue, and reattempt another time. We cannot stop trying to change.

To me, the speech that Teddy Roosevelt delivered on April 23, 1910, captures this perfectly. It has come to be known as "The Man in the Arena."

> It is not the critic who counts; not the man who points out how the strong man stumbles, or where the doer of deeds could have done them better. The credit belongs to the man who is actually in the arena, whose face is marred by dust and sweat and blood; who strives valiantly; who errs, who comes short again and again, because there is no effort without error and shortcoming; but who does actually strive to do the deeds; who knows great enthusiasms, the great devotions; who spends himself in a worthy cause; who at the best knows in the end the triumph of high achievement, and who at the worst, if he fails, at least fails while daring greatly, so that his place shall never be with those cold and timid souls who neither know victory nor defeat.

Change is inevitable. Will we be on the better side or, the worse side of change? Doing nothing always puts you on the worst side of change. The real answer is to embrace the needed changes by working together toward a common solution. Doing something with the help of others gives us a real chance to be on the better side of change. Even if the change didn't get the intended result, the best leaders just make another change until we get it right for all of us and each of us.

Out with the stagnating politics and in with new centrist politics

New ideas, new concerns, new products, and new institutions continue to move us forward. Yet our politics have stagnated, failing to keep pace with our fears, desires, and our changing circumstances. As in the past, there come to be significant times when old laws must be rewritten, eliminated, or replaced with new legislation that accommodate new situations and circumstances to protect while moving forward the line between our individual and our collective freedoms. Today is one of those times.

Time moves forward, but we are moving back because of our stagnating politics. We cannot afford to let some of our nonpolitical institutions, new products, new ideas, or new concerns decide our collective fate as a nation. Politically we must keep up with the new. We desperately need a new type of politician who understands today's fast-paced and changing world, and we must help them get elected. Our democratic system is all we have to preserve our collective and our individual lives and freedoms from divisive and stagnating politics.

Out with the old economic and business leadership model and In with a new true dynamic and connected economic and business leadership model

Again, time continues to move ahead. Certainly, we have learned many things about business leadership and our economy over the last 250 years. And yet Big Business, similar to Big Politics, is repeating over and over again the same major economic mistakes.

At the end of the 19th century, many citizens and immigrants did backbreaking labor never to find anything remotely resembling the American Dream. Life for struggling workers began to change in the early years of the 20th century only to fall on its face in 1929 with the stock market crash. Closing in on 200 years since our first bout with industrialization, almost half of our citizens are stuck in a never-ending cycle of life barely above poverty.

What is wrong with our business leadership? Most of today's Big Business leaders, again similar to yesterday, believe that the struggles faced by so many of us have nothing to do with them. I say, it has *everything* to do with them. Similar to Big Politics, we desperately need Big Business leaders who know they are responsible to each of us and all of us, not only themselves and stockholders.

Chapter 3

The Failure of Our Life System

"I've learned that 'making a living' is not the same as 'making a life.'"

— Maya Angelou

Our nonfunctioning Life System

Our Life System is comprised of:

- Society
- Economy
- Industry
- Education
- Our Democracy

> We must require our top-level leadership in both Big Business and Big Politics to build stronger connections between all five pieces of our Life System.

Only when these five elements are working together will all of us have the gifts promised by our country's founding fathers. At the moment, the connections of these parts of the Life System to one another are loose at best and miserably failing at worst. We must require our top-level leadership in both Big Business and Big Politics to build stronger connections between all five pieces of our Life System.

The most significant factors currently rendering our Life System nonfunctional are:

1. The world has changed significantly in the last several decades, linking humanity and the planet together physically and technologically. But We the People have failed to recognize completely that change and the potentially radical and detrimental effect on our future...as well as its opportunity to positively change our world forever.

2. Our current system of top-level leadership rewards those with superior leadership skills far too well, often leading to a God complex (narcissistic) leadership mentality, "My way is the only way."

3. Top-level narcissistic leadership is motivated by power and greed, leading to fear-based control leadership, self-serving solutions, and corruption.

4. The top-level institutions of Big Politics and Big Business operate from an unconnected silo mentality—one-size solutions fit all—rather than working together to provide optimal solutions for all when the diversity of the served population crosses borders, incomes, and needs.

5. Top-level institutions of Big Politics and Big Business exist in a competitive, winner-take-all environment,

creating many barriers to optimal solutions to over-whelming problems.

6. Since top-level institutional problems are overwhelming and success is difficult at the top levels of Big Politics and Big Business, solutions are not easily implemented—often short-term rather than long-term, incomplete, and need ongoing revision. Due to the system's competitive nature, upgrading occurs only intermittently and becomes more costly in time, money, and life itself.

7. Finally, the current Big Business economic model, profit over people, is driving inferior and detrimental decisions by Big Business and Big Politics relative to the ongoing health and security of all of us, and unfortunately, the longevity of humanity and the planet.

We must no longer be the roadblock to solutions to catastrophic problems

We the People are allowing top-level leaders to shirk their responsibility for us and our planet when it comes to all-encompassing life-changing crisis events. Let me explain.

Many of the past's major crises could have been avoided, limited, or attacked with much less impact on us with a lot more futuristic strategizing and planning. Over the last one and a half centuries, in almost all cases of significant crisis events and the connected life-changing human hardship, the signs of impending doom were not unforeseen. The Civil War, World War I and World War II, the stock market crash of 1929, the Vietnam War, 9/11, the 2008 housing bubble economic crash, and even the Covid-19 virus pandemic (not the specific virus but a virus pandemic). Many of our top-level leaders and/or their subordinate associates or outside experts predicted the impending catastrophic events.

In almost all cases, We the People just ignored the warning and hoped the problem would go away. We didn't want to get involved, or we believed the doom predictors were "crying wolf," or we believed Our Government or Big Business and its technology of the time would save us.

We are often the roadblock to solutions to catastrophic problems. We just don't want our lives to change. Accordingly, our politicians, our governments, and our largest businesses get our pass to do nothing. We the People of the U.S. and the world must no longer be the potential reason for our own and the planet's demise.

Going forward, we need to accept that all things in life change. When our top-level leadership—and our scientists and other experts— say we have a significant all-humanity and planetary problem, we must demand their action to immediately develop a strategy for avoiding it, limiting it, or attacking it. We can't accept "no strategy" for this type of problem. The planet is smaller because we are all connected to everywhere and everyone. Therefore every significant problem is global and must be solved globally because the cost of failure is equal to the value in lives.

How the God complex of top-level leadership causes disconnect of our Life System

Our former president, Donald Trump, is the epitome of the God complex, but he is not the only one to fall victim to its jaws. Almost everyone who attains the presidency of the U.S. has trappings of it. Additionally, everyone who reaches the presidency of any of our major corporations has those same trappings. The fact is that we want them to have that type of quality, along with many other qualities. We want them to be sure of their decisions because every decision they make affects us in some way or another.

A second undeniable fact is if we do not see some narcissistic quality in them, it's unlikely that he or she will get our vote. Whether citizens, board members, or stockholders, they must show confidence that borders on infallibility.

With all of that said, we must see other qualities that offset their narcissistic tendencies. Otherwise, the disconnect in our Life System will continue. Top-level leaders must be able to show the empathy side of their personalities for future leadership positions. If that side of their nature is missing, it is up to us to bypass them for top-level leadership positions. Narcissism without empathy is a recipe for disaster when it comes to making important decisions.

The presidency of the U.S. or the presidency of a major corporation are not the only positions that fall victim to narcissism. Up-and-coming stars in politics and business are all subjected to the power-and-greed dynamics of their opportunities. Many have succumbed to the never-ending overwhelming possibilities of power and greed. Everyone with leadership responsibility must hold their narcissism in check with the empathy side of their personality.

How the silo mentality of top leadership causes disconnect of our Life System

There are two ways to achieve success while in command. The first is control...often complete control where the leader makes all of the decisions about almost everything. The military is an example of this type of leadership at the lowest levels. Everyone is assigned tasks and a job and executes the functions and job as assigned. No deviation is allowed without the approval of the leader.

> We must have a system that does not operate in a silo.

As you move up the ladder, the second command model comes more into play even in the military. This command model is a blend of autonomy, consensus/collaboration, cooperation, coordination, and control. The subordinate is assigned a task but given a fair amount of flexibility in achieving it—could be time, could be process, could be wide open, but the goal must be completed within some time frame. In addition to the subordinate's assignment, he/she collaborates with a group working on the larger project in which he/she has integration responsibility. This type of command structure leader is more of an advisor, reviewer, motivator, and final decision-maker. He/she is looking for his/her subordinates to find their way through the project within the given structure and ultimate objective.

Why is this command structure distinction important?

The first command structure, complete control, is suitable for routine processes where deviation is not wanted or needed. The second is the best structure for solving problems of the future...where solutions are currently unknown, but significant realizable outcomes are possible given other current knowledge. As a country and a world, our governments and our largest businesses operate too much in the first scenario. This is odd for the level of responsibility our largest businesses and governments have for us people.

The second command structure, collaboration and cooperation, has an important element that is most often missing in our largest businesses and government. It is the element of connection to a group. At the highest business and government levels, the group is our Life System, all five institutions: society, economy, industry, education, and our democracy.

We must have a system that does not operate in a silo. We must force the connection to all Life System institutions. At top-level leadership, we need leaders who create institutional and organizational environments using the above second command structure that connects people and solutions to our significant world issues.

For Big Politics, the silo mentality is undermining solutions to issues like health care cost and access; the never-ending cycle of poverty; safety threatened by global warming disasters and water pollution; the security of a reasonably paid job; and equal opportunities for a good education, to name just a few lingering issues.

For Big Business, the silo mentality manifests itself in "profit matters more than customers, employees, or the communities" and its narrow focus on only what it currently does.

Standing on the outside of these two institutions, it's relatively easy to see the reasons for their failure. Both Institutions, because of their remote positions, conflicts within their operating systems, and their competitive environment, have very little ability to effect significant change without substantial risk to themselves or the political party or the business's perceived profitability and market. Thus the standard operating procedure...business as usual.

The silo mentality in Big Politics

Congress, the president, and the federal government and its agencies represent the whole country. However, the whole country is vast—many states, many cities, some urban, some rural, some low income some high income. The needs of the diversity of the population everywhere are all over the board. The mind-set is: "I don't know your state; I barely know mine." Members of Congress want what's best for the area he/she represents. Complicating this is the fact that the president and members of Congress come from one of two political parties, both with, at this time, totally different agendas and strategies for solutions. It is a wonder any legislation gets done, ever.

But we are out of time. Like never before, we must have a unifying leadership commonality for the foundation of legislating and a connecting process that brings all of our Life System components together to create optimal solutions for our overwhelming problems.

The silo mentality in Big Business

Once a business becomes a mega-corporation with revenues and profits in the billions, it often has millions of customers worldwide. Unfortunately, the mega-corporations are motivated more by revenue and profit goals than by their employees and customers' welfare. Everything revolves around stability: planned slow growth and continued profit increases. There is nothing wrong with stability...unless it slows or stops real innovation. We the People need you Big Business leaders to act like you did when you first began. We need your vision of the future…not just your company's future, but the world's future, and your push to connect everything to everything to make the world better than one company can make it. In other words, we need your help to restore our Life System connections.

To do that, we need to change your current funding mechanism revolving around quarterly profits to a new way of thinking.

The missing connection

The optimal solution fixes for many of the world's significant problems will continue to elude us citizens, customers, and employees until we bridge the chasm that currently separates the interested parties: Big Business, Big Politics, Big Government, and We the People.

Let's use global warming as an example. Global warming is the disaster that has been growing as a threat to our survival for decades, yet we have done just about nothing to slow or stop the increasing temperature of the planet. Individual big businesses have created solutions on some fronts in this fight, but so far, there has been no slowing. The planet's temperature is increasing even faster than earlier predictions indicated.

Big Business is failing in its attempt at a solution to this significant issue because of the connection failure between it and Big Politics, Big Government, and We the People. Slowing global warming is also in conflict with the profit motive. To be successful, an individual big business, whether working on global warming or any other significant problem, can only be a minor player in the overall solution due to its need to generate profits.

No one organization can solve any of these issues, and thus we must remove the silo mentality, remoteness, and competitiveness from the solution process. We must connect our big businesses to our most significant global problems by connecting the solution process to other big businesses involved in solutions and connecting them to Big Politics, Big Government, and We the People. All of these institutions, including us, must be engaged in the collaborative solution process.

The need for long-term goals and strategies

Big Politics and Big Business must begin to look at their objectives as long-term—not here-and-now goals and strategies but permanent and lifetime goals and strategies. We must abandon obstructionism in politics as a strategy/goal and short-term stock prices in business as a strategy/goal. Both Big Politics and Big Business will probably argue that these are not their strategies or goals, but history suggests otherwise.

One example of misaligned goals is using stock price increases as a significant feature of CEO compensation packages. We have seen many business examples of one CEO building a company's stock price by acquiring business units by leveraging (borrowing to acquire other business) for the benefit of his compensation. Then watch the next CEO sell them off to stop the bleeding, often to increase the stock price and his compensation.

In politics, we see the same behavior around the Affordable Care Act (Obamacare) and Supreme Court nominees; political positions pushed through on a partisan basis only—Affordable Care Act by the Democrats and Supreme Court justices by Republicans. Both are only widening the gap of an already divided nation.

Neither of these examples brings together any kind of long-term sustained positive growth for business or our country, and certainly not for us. At best, today's politics bring about the political stagnation of division we have seen over the past several decades. At worst, they perpetuate the rapid decline of our democracy due to partisan, fear-based attack politics that further divide our country. In business, the absolute and singular drive for short-term profit drives stock price but does not serve its customers.

When Big Business fights vigorously with millions of dollars and legions of lobbyists against any restrictions to its perceived due profits, the broader community of all of us is sacrificed. In recent years, we have seen the quest for profit far exceeding the preservation of our democracy. Several information technology giants allowed robot programs to propagate false information about our politics, further dividing our country. With interest rates at record lows, several mega-companies have taken on vast amounts of debt. Now is the time to borrow for the long term. But the debt was not for investment in thousands of jobs for new products or projects but, for the most part, to buy back its stock. Once again, the increase in stock price significantly benefits only two stakeholders: the executive team and stockholders.

Like Donald Trump's corporate tax cut of 2017, where We the People were supposed to benefit from thousands of new well-paid jobs, we, again, got no jobs from these borrowed funds, only stock buybacks to further increase the wealth of executives and stockholders.

We will reconnect our Life System components only by stopping this shortsighted, short-term, limited benefiting behavior. It serves only *some* of us. It does not even serve businesses or political parties. The leadership of Big Business and Big Politics must adopt long-term goals and implement strategies that will move the country and their businesses forward like never before.

We must convince Big Politics and Big Business to work together…but not in the economic partnership they have created over the last four decades. They must genuinely work together for the betterment of the people of the world. Big Politics and Big Business must put aside the money motive—special favors for increased business profit in exchange for campaign funding. The focus of legislation must be the problem to be solved as it relates to the people, each of us and all of us. Only then will our Life System be complete.

Part II

True Leadership Leads for the Benefit of All of Us and Each of Us, Not Just for Some of Us

Chapter 4

True Leadership Defined

"You are not here merely to make a living. You are here in order to enable the world to live more amply, with greater vision, with a finer spirit of hope and achievement. You are here to enrich the world, and you impoverish yourself if you forget the errand."

— *Woodrow Wilson*

Our new leadership model

"We the People," says it all.

A True Leader is driven by his or her commitment to their responsibility to each of us, and for all of us, without regard to position or job, organization, or specific life circumstance.

Years ago, we had a political slogan, "Power to the people." Who did we mean by the word "people"? Did it mean only those with the same skin color as me? Did it mean only those whose religion was the same as mine? Did it mean only those who were the same sex as me? Did it mean only those who were as rich as I was? Did it mean only those who lived in my neighborhood, or city, or state? Did it mean only those who believed everything I believed?

After winning an election, many politicians have promised to govern for all of the people, not just those who supported them. If those promises were fulfilled, why has important legislation been stuck for decades?

We have also heard many legislators say the business of government is slow and deliberate for a reason. In truth, they don't want the other party to reverse or significantly change poorly drafted legislation once they are in power.

In today's fast-paced world, We the People can't wait on stalled legislation that negatively affects our daily and future lives. We need legislators who understand the difference between yesterday's time frame and today's. Therefore, We the People must have legislators adopt a nonpartisan perspective on legislative solutions. We need them to understand that We the People rule, and all of us and each of us are We the People. We can't afford to continue down the path of slow to no legislation. Otherwise, democracy, and maybe the world, will not survive much longer. We the People must elect legislators who get this fact: that all of us and each of us are We the People.

Yesterday's solutions will not work

During my forty years in business, I worked in many industries: construction, retail, franchising, service, manufacturing, banking, insurance, restaurants, and others. Many of the business owners were trying to save their businesses or improve their profits. I wanted them to understand that their business's focus was the business itself and not the product or production process.

Many of these business owners did not want to change to this mentality. They loved what they produced and how they produced it. But other businesses survived by embracing a culture change. Change always starts at the top. The CEO had to understand that getting the best results required caring about each employee, each customer, and each supplier all of the time. Peak performance requires that *all* of us care about *each* of us all of the time. Leadership matters every time we impact the lives of others for good or bad.

Those business owners or managers who succeeded were willing to share the leadership responsibility with others, meaning they gave up the misconception that they were the only ones with the best ideas. They also realized that their leadership, and the business, required continuous progress monitoring corrective change. Everything changes rapidly today—technology, employees, customers, products, services, and the list goes on.

In the bigger picture, the world and We the People are the business itself. But we need to change the culture and the process to save our world, and the production process itself isn't giving us what we need.

True Leaders connect each of us and all of us

A True Leader is driven by a commitment to his or her responsibility to each of us and for all of us without regard to position or job, organization, or life circumstance. Above all, a True Leader knows that this is not a struggle between each of us as individuals or groups of us as represented by some organization or peer group, but a struggle within ourselves to recognize, understand, promote, and never diminish the importance and connection to each of us and all of us in the fight for our democracy and our humanity.

> We are all part of a global family, and we will succeed as a family only by putting the needs of the family above the needs of specific individuals or groups.

"Each of us" simply means that no one gets left behind. "All of us" simply means we all share in the benefits and the costs.

An easy analogy is family. A child is born with a disability to a family with other children. The True Leaders, Mom and Dad, will lead by making the hard decisions necessary to connect *all* children to the family. They will bind the family together in love by sharing the benefits, costs, and challenges of a family who has a child with a disability.

Now, all we have to do is expand this analogy. We are all part of a global family, and we will succeed as a family only by putting the needs of the family above the needs of specific groups. "We" is "all of us," so if "some of us" have a problem that needs fixing, "all of us" have a problem that needs fixing.

Unfortunately, today many worldwide democratic leaders use separation tactics to win favor with only part of their electorate. According to these divisive leaders, political and otherwise, "freedom" is often used to justify actions taken by our government or other organizations and institutions to favor one or more individuals, organizations, or institutions over another. This is a gross misuse of the word "freedom." Whenever freedom is used as justification for a case or cause, another word in our democracy is ignored. That word is "equal." Often these words conflict in the interpretation of actions taken by one party against another party or legislation promoting a specific outcome for future conflicts.

The misuse of "freedom" by Big Business

The word "freedom" should apply only to people: freedom from tyranny and bondage of governments. However, in our country's history, the definition of "freedom" has been extended to businesses—almost always Big Business—in their conflicts against humanity. Our courts and legislation have seen fit to give these non-similar parties Equal standing when it comes to freedom. Big businesses are always fighting in lobbying and legislation for their freedom to impose tyranny and bondage on people. We just don't call it tyranny and bondage. Big Business calls it "fairness and price containment." It's really about profit for their stockholders and the senior executives.

Big Business, with its freedom to impose its version of "equal" manifests itself in many forms:

- Health care issues—cost and access.

- Privacy issues—data gathering "for our benefit."

- Reductions in regulations—limiting product liability, limiting wage increases, limiting liability for age discrimination and employee class-action suits, and work hours and conditions.

Big Business's argument has always been that they must limit their production cost so they can produce something needed by us citizens for a reasonable price. But why should Big Business have this freedom? Independent small business, maybe; Big Business, no. Big Business should no longer get the freedom to choose profits over people.

Why do we citizens allow this from Big Business? Big Business leaders know that often the cost of what they are avoiding comes at great cost later—sickness, pollution, clean up, etc. Still, they shift the cost and the legislative focus to the future, giving legislators short-term cover and reelection because the cost consequences are kicked down the road.

We voters don't pay close enough attention to this bait-and-switch tactic. Do we really want our children to pay the cost? It's time we own up to the responsibility we have to future generations. Big Business and Congress must stop kicking the cost can down the road. If we don't, we will be in for a very rocky next several decades…and maybe a point of no return.

The misuse of "freedom" by Big Politics

Big Politics has created group disparities in its treatment of all of us with regard to our freedom and equality. Some laws appear to be easy to apply uniformly on the surface, but the enforcement or application process can create uneven outcomes due to our separating circumstances and biases. The drug enforcement laws of the past are still wreaking havoc on our Black population. Our immigration laws have the effect of targeting anyone of color. Our education system fails to produce an equal education process for the poor and children of color, both in our inner cities and rural America.

True Leaders in both Big Business and Big Politics must lead like the mom and dad of a child with a disability—the analogy I mentioned earlier. They will recognize, understand, promote, and never diminish the importance and connection to each of us and all of us, whether for us or future generations. Although challenging, a True Leader knows they cannot duck this responsibility but takes it head-on with truth and sincerity.

True Leadership is the process of leading, not the position you hold. When deciding or recommending anything, a True Leader considers the consequences of the decision or recommendation on all of us and each of us, not the benefits or costs for some of us. As discussed earlier, all of us and each of us are connected. Therefore, if the consequences of the decision or recommendation are positive (benefiting) for all of us and each of us, a True Leader would recommend it. If the decision or endorsement implications are negative (costing) for all of us and each of us, a True Leader would not recommend it.

Benefits and costs do not equate to money. Money is a tool (like a hammer for a carpenter) to make trading transactions easier, nothing more and nothing less, unless we give it power in our choice of leaders. Money's influence will be discussed elsewhere throughout the book. As I use it here, benefits are the positive consequences (outcomes) of a proposed change solution (strategy) on all of us and each of us. As I use it here, costs are the negative consequences (outcomes) of a proposed change solution (strategy) on all of us and each of us. Remember, "We" is all of us. Therefore, if some of us have a problem that needs fixing, all of us have a problem that needs fixing. We have a problem. We need a change. Will the proposal fix the problem or not? Or will it move us closer to the ultimate solution or not?

In politics, fairness to all, considering differing financial circumstances in the quest for fairness to all of us, is reasonable. When it comes to our humanity, we are all equal. Therefore the provided benefit to each of us is equal to the benefit provided to the rest of us. On the other hand, the out-of-pocket price for an equivalent benefit may cost some more than others due to their financial circumstances. Equivalent benefit defined is a combination of the two lowest levels of Maslow's Hierarchy of Needs (more about this later) and the second paragraph to the Declaration of Independence and the Preamble to the Constitution.

> Life Benefit = air, food, water, shelter, safety/security, energy, information/communication, education, and health care = work/school.

See additional discussion on this all-important equation in significantly more detail in Chapter 9.

Our missing responsibility for the choice and measurement of top-level leaders

In the past, when borders mattered, physical or on a map, and people formed a group, a country, a race, a religion, a lineage, leadership involved only the group. In today's world, borders are gone. Technology and air travel have wiped them off the map. They provide no safety and security or commonality of highest purpose when, in any one of several ways, someone or some perceived group—from next door or around the world—can have a devastating effect on our life or millions of lives around our country and the world.

However, we have not yet grasped the full extent of our global reality changes and, accordingly, our new and much broader responsibility. We the People of the world now have an obligation to ourselves and everyone else on the planet to hold accountable the top-level leaders of Big Politics and Big Business.

We the People must begin to hold leaders accountable to us, not to business or the rich, and for all of us, not some or few of us. Our legislation and policy changes must begin to reflect the transition to this model. We must show our leaders of Big Politics and Big Business that this is now a fundamental and foundational goal for future leadership positions.

Our own leadership responsibilities

Today we see the symptoms of leadership failure at the highest levels, the divisiveness in our political system, and politics around the world. But it's not just our politics that needs the new leadership definition. The new leadership definition must apply to our business leaders, our religious leaders, institutional and organizational leaders, and virtually all leadership.

Notably, we must also hold ourselves as individuals accountable to the new leadership definition. If we don't, then we won't succeed in holding leaders at the top accountable.

Many of us have lost our truth and sincerity about why we do what we do. We started our working careers with high hopes for changing the world…and now suddenly find ourselves grinding out a day's living instead of changing the world. We are human. Life is a balancing act between our daily lives and our commitment to the broader community.

We all have lives that are much smaller than the big picture. However, still, we can adopt the definition of True Leadership. A True Leader is driven by his or her commitment to their responsibility to each of us and for all of us without regard to position or job, organization, or specific life circumstance.

Sometimes global disasters can help to refocus our attention on the big picture. Our response to the Covid-19 pandemic is a good example. The virus allowed every one of us to be heroes by acting in various ways to protect and help everyone around us. Most of us stayed home; some of us had to work; some of us put our lives on the line every minute of every day during the crisis. Some of us became Guinea pigs for drug trials, and almost all of us sacrificed much of our daily income to save someone else's life. There are no better examples of True Leaders than all of us.

This is the story that finally brought everything together for me. Early in the Covid-19 pandemic, many doctors and nurses had to quit their jobs to go to where help was needed most: New York City. These doctors and nurses were told, "if you leave, you may not have a job when you come back." They left anyway because they believed it was the right thing to do. Imagine the courage that it took to do that. Imagine the courage it took each one of us to do our part to save the life of someone unknown to us.

We need that type of courage from our top-level political and business leaders. They should put their jobs on the table to support people. Most don't need to put their income on the table. Most have more than enough for the remainder of their lives. We should not have to force them to do the right thing.

Big Business should ask that legislation be drafted to do just that, and Big Politics should immediately make it law. Later in the book, I'll outline how to do it. We cannot wait any longer.

Chapter 5

The Foundation for True Leadership

"Tolerance and compassion are active, not passive states, born of the capacity to listen, to observe and to respect others."

— *Indira Gandhi*

The role of ethics and morality in True Leadership

Since humans began walking the earth, we have been searching for the answers to our physical situation. We call this process "science," and it has taught us much about nature and the world in which we live.

But we have learned less about who we are and why we are so different from one another in our world of thought and how we treat each other. This comes down to a question of ethics and morality.

We have been struggling with this for millennia. Our religions have tried in vain to give us an understanding of who we are. In doing so, they created a separation between us in many forms: geography, skin color, rich and poor, man and woman, and especially theology—who's right and who's wrong. Our nation-states have extended that separation significantly by drawing imaginary lines in the dirt about which we cannot cross or let others cross.

Today our nation-states force us to back a political party to have any influence at all over the state of our world. Also, in today's world, our careers and the related business and/or organizations we belong to have an extreme influence on our state of mind. Career and job are incredibly influential in our thinking since our livelihood depends on it. Finally, at the most basic level, our friends and family have the most influence on our lives.

Couple those rules with our intellectual differences, and we have a real mess when it comes to discerning which parts of our integrated life we are going to follow.

Unfortunately, the influence these various groups have over us tends to water down the connection we have to each of us and all of us. We must cut that peripheral influence and reconnect to all of our brothers and sisters.

I think of it this way: we are all the children of God or nature no matter who we are, what we believe, where we live, where we work, or whose child or friend we are. Accordingly, we are all connected.

With that in mind, we are faced with a question humans have been struggling with for millennia: What is right or wrong?

I believe our decision-making process, and often our opinions, come from three areas of our human development: personality, upbringing, and life experiences. Our education forms our ability to analyze and develop our technical life skills to balance these three areas of our development.

We are born with a hardwired personality, and our basic personality can't be changed. With education and work, we can better understand our personality, but we cannot change its core. If you're an introvert, you can't snap your fingers or take classes that will turn you into an extrovert. The important thing is to make an effort to understand who we are and fight against anything in our personality that doesn't work as well as we'd like. That understanding, and the further development of our personality, often takes a lifetime. Shortcutting personality development can and does create leaders who are stuck in their youth's success—a significant reason for our top-level leadership debacle.

Upbringing comes from our childhood parental influence. There are generally two possible influence patterns: 1) strict, in which rules dominate decisions and actions, and 2) nurturing, in which encouragement and reinforcement of behavior drives decisions and actions. Both influence systems can work well with some children and not with others. The undeveloped child's personality, already beginning to take shape, will generally determine which type of parental influence will work best with each child. However, that's not the way families operate. Children are all raised similarly. Accordingly, the young adult version of the child may rebel against their childhood experience or embrace their childhood experience in their view of the world. Why is this important? It begins to show the combining effects of personality and upbringing on future decisions and opinions.

Combining personality and upbringing has a significant impact on future decisions and opinions about how we treat others. Now we add life experiences from family, friends, ethnicity, school, work, religion, and almost anything else to the mix of personality and upbringing. We are thus creating even more confusion in our decision-making process. The level of influence on our lives comes from personal relationships and experiences inside these connecting activities. The deeper the relationships, the more the experiences influence our decisions and opinions. The shallower the relationships, the less likely we will form a substantive decision or judgment.

In today's world, our top-level leaders and their decisions are front and center because of our electronically wired society. We continuously judge their ability to lead because of the vast array of information presented. The sheer amount of data requires our ability to use our education to balance our entire picture of the leader's leadership skills relative to our leadership foundational principles.

True Leadership foundational principles

I believe that True Leaders should:

- Lead from love, not fear.

- Value differences among people.

- Have the desire to serve others.

- Believe in fairness and equality.

- Understand the importance of creating without harming.

- Know how to teach and encourage rather than demand.

- Be willing to accept responsibility.

> We must not allow our fears and the fears of our leaders to be the motivation to continue to repeat our bad decisions of the past.

Lead from love, not fear

Leading from fear leads to resentment, disdain, and conflict—often sustained conflict.

We must not allow our fears and the fears of our leaders to be the motivation to continue to repeat our bad decisions of the past. Instead, our love of our neighbors, in the form of hope, must be our motivational support for our leaders' actions to move all of us and each of us, positively and significantly, into the future.

Some readers will question my use of the word "love" in the context of leadership. So let me clarify.

Love has many forms. We can say that we love the music of Beethoven or the Beatles. We can say that we love road trips or ocean cruises. We can say that we love pickup trucks or sports cars. The deepest love we feel is usually for people around us: our spouse or significant other, our children, our parents and siblings, and our closest friends. We call this intense, heartfelt connection to another person "love."

But can we love somebody we don't even know? Most of us can feel sympathy and compassion for someone who has suffered a heartbreaking loss, even if we don't know the person. We can feel respect for someone who devotes his or her life to helping others, even if we don't know that person. But can we actually feel "love" for somebody we don't know, even if we have respect and/or empathy for them?

You're probably thinking, *No, that isn't possible. I can't love somebody I don't even know and have never met.*

> False leaders know they can use fear rhetoric to stoke our tribal instincts about others, essentially using our diversity to divide us.

I believe you can! You just have to let yourself do it. That may require some reprogramming. Almost from birth, the way we feel toward others has been impacted by our parents, education, life experiences, and even genetics. From an early age, we were told to be wary of strangers. For many of us, as we grew older, this "be wary of strangers" concept expanded to include anyone who looked, acted, or thought in ways different from our own. Much of this has been due to separation tactics practiced by leaders of groups we belong to, such as political parties and religious organizations.

False leaders know they can use fear rhetoric to stoke our tribal instincts about others, essentially using our diversity to divide us. Fear rhetoric comes in many forms: skin color, nationality, religion, tribal sects, and many others. The result is we don't trust anyone who isn't exactly like us in appearance or beliefs.

In fact, though, we're all together in this family of humanity. Each of us is somebody's daughter or somebody's son. Each of us contends with daily struggles of one kind or another. And most of us are willing to step up and help someone in distress, even if that person is a "stranger." Think about the doctors and nurses who risked their own lives and wellbeing to help care for those struck down by Covid-19. Think of Mohammad Salman Hamdani, a Pakistani-American who saw the burning World Trade Center on September 11 and lost his life while saving others from the inferno. Think of Ryan Cox, who was killed in the 2019 mass shooting at a Virginia Beach municipal building. Ryan could still be alive today. He had found shelter with a few coworkers but chose to leave the shelter and save others instead. Think of aid workers who leave their comfortable lives in the United States to help the impoverished in dangerous, war-torn places far from home.

What is it that inspires someone to risk his or her life to help a stranger? It has to be more than compassion or respect for that stranger. It takes an immediate grasp of the fact that, despite our differences, we're all part of a world family. It takes a genuine love for others, even strangers.

We need this kind of love for others in our top-level leaders of Big Business and Big Politics. We need leaders who care about making sure everyone can have health care, clean water, job security, education, access to information, and safe working environments that we, all of us, deserve. We need leaders who condemn hate speech and actions. We need leaders who see everyone, regardless of race, gender, religion, age, or ethnicity, as part of our family.

This kind of True Leadership is within our grasp, but we don't yet have it. What we have are too many false leaders who ignore the daily struggles of our world family. We are all now in the midst of a top-level leadership crisis. We need our highest levels of leadership to love us all. Otherwise, our very democracy is threatened. More than anything else, democracy celebrates our collective diversity to accomplish the serious and significant task of positive human change. The main reason for democracy's potential failure is the fear of our neighbor.

We are at a tipping point. We will either slide into a collapse of democracy, or we must begin to see many of our political leaders for what they are: false, fearmongering leaders in politics only for personal gain and power. We must fight hard for True Leaders who will fight for each of us and all of us, and promote hope instead of fear in our quest for serious and significant positive human change.

Personality and the value of diversity

Can you imagine a world in which everyone had the same personality? At first, that may seem like a good thing. However, from a work perspective, nothing would get done. We would all want to do the same job or a very narrow range of careers. We need a wide variety of personalities to get all our world's vital work done.

Interestingly, and very irritating to me, is our current data-driven fixation on pigeonholing people into another job precisely the same as their last one. This is so not required or needed by our future economy. Each person's personality allows for a wide variety of occupations, not just one. Success or failure in any profession can come from experience, but, from my observation, it's a person's desire to do the work that drives success. A candidate for a new position should not be eliminated for lack of exact work experience, because more often than not, required training for a new job is relatively minor when the person is motivated.

Whenever hiring, after reviewing a person's résumé, I only asked one significant question: "Why do you want this job?" In other words, I was looking for their motivation to do the work. Motivation is so much more than mere experience in many, many jobs. I have a good friend who started his career as a salesperson. He sold for many years and was quite successful, but he burnt out at about age forty. He went back to school to become a nurse and has been in nursing in a hospital setting for almost thirty years. He loves his new profession and will continue to do it until he can't.

Currently, in this ever-changing world, we need a wide variety of new workers. Many of those new workers could, with a little training, come from jobs that no longer exist.

Although it may seem natural to think that most of us would want to be the boss, the reality is, most of us don't. Managing people almost always creates conflict, and most of us don't like conflict. Our shying away from people-management partially comes from our personality but also our life experiences.

Personality, again along with family and life experience, tends to split us into two significant but important groups: those who look to the future and those who focus on the "here and now." All of us have a little of both, but we tend to gravitate to one or the other, especially in our work. The future-thinker group is significantly smaller than the here-and-now group. The future-thinker group tends to be top-level leaders, but not always. The here-and-now group tends to be technical problem-solvers, but not always. Just as we need workers for everything we need in our economy, we need both of these groups to work together closely to change the world for the better. The future-thinker group will give us the direction we must go, the dreams yet to be realized, and the disasters to avoid. The here-and-now group must use their technical skills and knowledge to create the required actual products to save ourselves and our planet from the catastrophe on the horizon, and those products must be produced in advance of their required need.

How does all this talk about personality and motivation fit into a book about True Leadership?

Balancing logic and empathy

Here's the answer: we need millions of good True Leaders, but they must want to lead multiple people in varying work settings, including Big Business and Big Politics. They must be able to lead both the future-thinker group and the here-and-now group.

Leaders in politics and business generally have personalities that connect to these professions. For the most part, politicians are not typically from the Big Business world, and Big Business men and women are not politicians. Of course, there are a few exceptions, such as Donald Trump. Usually, politicians, because of their personality, are driven to serve people. Because of their personality, Big Business men and women are driven to produce something on a vast scale. In the big picture, there is not much difference between them. Both are driven to a high level of success by their belief in the contributing value of their accomplishments...politicians doing for the people, and business men and women for the producing organization.

Politicians must understand voters with significant differences on many issues and then balance those differences to create meaningful outcomes. Business men and women must coordinate the efforts of massive numbers of employees in the production process, all to make a significant amount of money. Most of us want careers with much less frustration because our personality does not want anything near that type of complication.

If Politicians and Big Business thrive on coordinating complicated things involving massive amounts of people, what are the reasons for their separate career direction? The answer is, again, in their personality. The personality of a typical business man or woman is driven by the logical elements in the process of creating a product. A typical politician's personality is driven by the empathetic elements of solving a problem for the people they serve.

> Over the last few decades and culminating with Donald Trump's election, our political process has deteriorated into a process where there is no balancing of logic and empathy.

Let's step back for a moment. As far as politicians are concerned, Republican politicians are much more likely to come from the business world than are Democratic politicians. Why? Republicans are much more likely to advocate for solutions that prioritize quantifiable outcomes, similar to how business men and women think. Their Democratic colleagues are much more likely to advocate for solutions prioritizing their constituents' severe and significant pain. Both

Republicans and Democrats generally attempt to balance both logic and empathy elements of their personalities to agree on solutions for society's problems.

Over the last few decades and culminating with Trump's election, our political process has deteriorated into a process where there is no balancing of logic and empathy. Division in our world is once again dominating our discourse and politics. Like our Big Politics and Big Business leaders, we are no longer balancing the logical and empathetic elements of our personalities. This is not right and not good for us and our world.

As discussed earlier, when talking about leadership in politics and Big Business, personality drives our career decisions. It also guides our life decisions and how we value and treat others.

Let me use the Covid-19 mask controversy to illustrate my concern. We were told for months that wearing a mask would prevent others from getting the virus. It would not protect us, but it would protect those around us. Early on, most of us wore masks, and our state and local governments—not federal—instituted policies for mask-wearing circumstances. The policies came and went in most areas and came again after many more got sick and many more died. Throughout this time, many refused to wear a mask. Donald Trump encouraged no mask-wearing by his own refusal to wear a mask.

Now let's get back to logic and empathy. There is no logic to not wearing a mask in the midst of this dangerous virus, given the statistical information presented to us on mask-wearing value in keeping others well. Accordingly, the only conclusion one can make is that anyone refusing to wear a mask had decided to abandon any empathy for the people they could infect by their behavior. This is equivalent to manslaughter in the case of a drunk driver killing someone...total disregard for someone else's life. It is not a question of freedom; it is a blatant disregard for someone other than you.

Some of us are not capable of this type of understanding; most of us are.

There will always be some of us who think "freedom means

I should be able to do anything I want." We, the rest of us, must elect True Leaders who consider all of us and each of us when making laws that keep us safe and secure—even a law that will include those who think mask-wearing is not macho and they should not have to wear one.

As the experts said early on, eliminating mask-wearing would not bring the economy back quicker, only slower. They were right again. Where was our True Leadership?

Serving others with fairness and equality

When it comes to life and fairness, we all received a different hand. We all have different appearances, distinct personalities, and gifts of various degrees that lead us to careers in as many jobs as it seems there are stars in the sky. Some of us were born with disabilities or significant illness, even if it does not show itself until later in life. Some of us were born with a body that doesn't match our mind. There are many other differences among us.

Most of these differences have to do with our DNA. We were born that way. But how we treat other people that aren't like us, is on us. Too many of us judge others and their life's circumstance as their own doing, as opposed to barriers the rest of us have created to impede their success.

I once worked for a check-cashing and payday loan company where all of the employees struggled with life. Almost all were women of color, all had children, and all had at most a high school degree. Most worked more than one job to make ends meet. They grew up in a similar home environment. And finally, all of them had a payday loan, by far the most expensive loan there is. They got that loan when something went wrong in their fragile life: a car repair, a large utility bill, a sick child. They needed $400 or $500; then they paid interest on the renewal of the loan every two weeks for virtually forever. None of them had time or money to change their life circumstance. But all of them were responsible; all showed up for work every day on time and worked hard. By the way, all of the customers of this business were in similar circumstances.

The problem here has nothing to do with resolve or responsibility. It has to do with circumstances, environments, and opportunities. Similar issues occur from a job loss, an addiction, severe illness, or anything creating an uncertain or fearful future for the affected individual. Most of us are not equipped with knowledge and support to move forward to handle unfortunate circumstances, even if we created them ourselves.

It's finally encouraging to see solutions taking shape in some of our prisons, schools, and communities. The problem is complex, so the answers are complex, but an essential piece of the solution is a mentorship mentality. Role models are needed to show and support the struggling that there is a path out of their circumstance. In other words, like parents, we must show them love and nurture, something that too often did not happen earlier in their lives.

Sadly, Big Business takes no responsibility for any of this, except for a little money around the edges. They could do much better. Currently, nonprofit organizations and governments support these programs.

Big Banks could get together and help create a significant process to help families in need, not only with money management but also with daycare, college opportunities, job opportunities, etc. With its need for well-educated employees and new growth opportunities, Big Business could spend significantly more money on education and training, similar to their research and development funding. I think our world would be surprised by the result of this type of investment. We need business leaders who understand the value of their employees, their customers, and their service to their community, not just their paychecks and their stock price.

The leadership failure in rural America

Rural America is another example of current leadership's failure to serve others with fairness and equality. Rural America has been suffering from little to no growth opportunity over the last several decades. I spent a fair amount of time consulting with small businesses in this sector.

As discussed earlier, rural America's economic problems were caused by poor political choices resulting in job transfers to cheaper foreign markets and advances in technology. But it's more complicated than that. Significant growth in our broader economy has been in information technology, health care, and oil and gas production. These are all highly specialized sectors, and the businesses involved in these industries need highly trained and skilled workforces. The education system in rural America has been slow to address this need, including the wider use of Internet technology, and has received no significant federal help.

> Many hardworking Americans have been left behind and are very angry because no one appears to care about them.

Big Business and Big Politics have not provided any significant assistance in either upgrading education or upgrading today's world's new required tools. Big Business does not think it's their problem, and Big Politics believes it can't afford it. Accordingly, good-paying jobs are hard to find in rural America, especially with the wrong education. Many have left the community, but the ones who have stayed are struggling to meet everyday needs. Voters in these regions blame the Democrats because they were the party of farmers and labor. However, Big Business, the acquirer of the former industries in the form of manufacturing, consolidated farming, and food production and retail in the form of groceries and other soft goods, are all paying less than a living wage to their workers.

These hardworking Americans have been left behind and are very angry because no one appears to care about them. Donald Trump's slogan to "Make America Great Again" has not solved this problem. The only solution is True Leadership change at Big Business and Big Politics, where We the People force them to work together for our benefit.

Create without harm

It seems as though there is a Big Business scandal at least monthly in today's world. In the last few years, we have heard of significant issues involving almost all Big Business industries: banking and investment banking, airplanes and airlines, social media, tech and telecom, media, pharma, tobacco and related, retail, transportation, autos, data management, utilities, oil and gas, mining, metals, health care, and the list goes on. Unfortunately, there is no industry untouched by the harm it has done to the lives of the customers and communities they serve and, in some cases, to the lives of their employees. Some are small issues, some catastrophic…life and death issues. Some matters are mistakes or an intentional rogue employee, but again, most are cultural and caused by poor leadership at the highest levels.

The unfortunate part of this is that no one at the most senior leadership levels is ever held personally responsible. The leaders of Big Business are paid very well. Their failure to lead from love, in which all of us and each of us are the reason for the business's existence, not the financial reward, should have consequences. After all, there is no business without employees, customers, and the community. We don't even need stockholders if there is nobody to make it, nobody to buy it, and no place to make it. Think about this at the next board meeting.

And yes, we need every industry to make this world a better place. We just need better leadership, True Leadership, to make the world even better.

Teach, don't demand

"Do as I say, not as I do."

My dad used to say this to me when I was a youngster. My dad was a navy medical corpsman as a young man. From that day on, I committed never to lead like that. It didn't make sense to me. Why would I do something different than the way my dad did it? There was no explanation, only a requirement to do it as he said.

Leading requires an explanation from the leader and an understanding of the instructions by the subordinate—or in my example, the child. Although I was never in the military, many friends who were have told me similar training stories to my dad's: "Do as I say, not as I do." This may not be a bad thing in the military. In battle, the commander has one responsibility; you have another. Both of your lives depend on quick commands and decisions to make it through the battle.

Most of life is not like the military, and accordingly, explanations at the time of the command are critical to culture and understanding. The explanations are essential in building bonds between coworkers and building the culture in any organization. True Leaders get this and are continually teaching the *Why's* to build bonds and culture.

Another vital lesson our military teaches every recruit: "You are not only responsible for yourself, but you are also responsible for everyone on your team, and everyone else, up to everyone in our country." Our military has fought many wars with that responsibility in mind. Many have died for it. That responsibility is still there today, and many in our military are still fighting for the rest of us. It seems to me that all of us should also be fighting for each other...the rest of us.

Accept responsibility

In today's world, most top leadership does not accept responsibility for any negative issues. Big Business always negotiates cash settlements with a caveat of no wrongdoing by either the company or its executive team. Additionally, top leadership never gets jail time for its role in harmful actions. Also, it seems that top leadership never knows about the company's negative issues. Even the deaths of customers, employees, and community members have little effect on top-level Big Business leaders or the company.

> The leaders of Big Business and Big Politics must be held accountable to each of us and all of us.

In today's politics, anything seems to be acceptable. Everything is a spin story. Party consensus is rare, only minimal compromise on crises or simple legislation. Legislation that solves today's problems, let alone tomorrow's, never gets anywhere.

This must change. The leaders of our most significant organizations, Big Business and Big Politics, must be held accountable to each of us and all of us. If they lead as we describe with each of us and all of us in mind, they should not have to worry about the negative consequences of their organization's actions or their own actions. There will no longer be the "profit trumps everything" mentality in Big Business, or the "next election campaign funding trumps everything" mentality in Big Politics. Leaders choosing not to lead for each of us and all of us should receive a punishment equal to their leadership role and compensation. Leadership in the transition to a new culture should not be held accountable for the past leadership team's misguided direction.

The preceding may seem harsh to many, but no True Leader should fear to lead for each of us and all of us. Leadership mistakes and accidents will happen. Still, leaders who build a culture of positive reinforcement and attempt to do their best need not fear any adverse consequences of their True Leadership, only positive outcomes.

Chapter 6

We Must Choose Top-Level True Leaders

"The greatest leader is not necessarily the one who does the greatest things. He is the one that gets the people to do the greatest things."

— *Ronald Reagan*

We must overcome fear if we are to choose our True Leaders

Many people promote themselves as leaders. However, now we can ask: Are they acting on behalf of all of us and each of us. Or are they working for themselves or only some of us?

Remember, we are We the People. We have the power to choose. Many of us feel helpless in that choice. We think the system is rigged against us. We believe that if we speak up, we will be shut down...or in the case of our workplace, we will be fired. We don't want to get involved for fear that we will anger our neighbors or family. We don't want to hear about the problems. We don't watch the news because it's about everything wrong in the world. For most of us, we just want the many significant problems in our world to go away.

This is due to fear. Our current leaders are using fear to keep us in our place. Bosses and political leaders have used gender, color, religion, origin, money, jobs, and anything else to keep us down. Too often, our political leaders use divisive strategy to pit us against each other on everything from health care, to global warming, to immigration, to world peace, to our economy, to jobs, to gun control, and the list goes on. In their never-ending insatiable desire to make more and more money for their leadership, Big Business is a cozy bedfellow in the political fearmongering by sponsoring ads and/or lobbying Congress for favorable treatment about anything that may affect their profit.

Top-level leaders in power have used this fear strategy since time began, and if we are to survive, we must call it out as something we will no longer tolerate in any form, at any time, with any leader.

We white people—primarily white men—can not deny our culpability in letting bad leaders pit us against each other. Nor should those who are the victims of past inhumanity and suffering forgive us or continue to accept this abhorrent leadership.

Our lower-income white voters fear losing jobs to immigrants and long-term loss of the white political majority. Our former president, Donald Trump, stoked both of these fears with his separation rhetoric, especially his immigration policy attempting to limit future nonwhite immigrant migration into the United States.

The solution to the immigration problem becomes simple if we adopt the proposed True Leadership definition. That's not to say it's an immediate solution, but if the True Leaders of our world attack the corruption, violence, and poverty in the migrants' home country, there would be no reason for anyone to migrate. Many will say this is unrealistic. I will say, "It's the only real solution to many of our problems." We, the free world, must begin to solve our world problems with long-term solutions, not short-term Band-Aids.

We, all of us and each of us, must unite in our common humanity

We, all of us and each of us, culpable and victims, must immediately unite with each other in our common humanity lest we fall short of saving our world and ourselves from our poor leadership choices. Our current world leaders have taken the bait of some of the worst leaders in history. We are all now seeing division around the world pitting people against people, countries against countries, religions against religions, men against women, and Big Business against every stakeholder except top-level leadership and stockholders.

We must begin to walk hand-in-hand together: black, white, brown, red, and yellow; Christian, Jewish, Muslim, Buddhist, Hindu, and all other religions and nonreligious; all people from all countries; all sexes and genders; everyone from everywhere. We must begin to see each other as humans, not some narrowing vision that lends fuel for unscrupulous leaders to separate us from each other. Although we may look different on the outside, we have all the same chemistry on the inside. Let's start seeing ourselves and each other from our inside vantage point. We must care about each of us and all of us. If we do care for each other, unscrupulous leaders will have no power over us.

We must see—and accordingly, our True Leaders must see—that all of us and each of us matter, no matter who we are, where we live, what language we speak, what religion we practice, or anything else.

Our whole world matters because it's the only one we have. We the People can't wait any longer for visionary True Leaders. We need them now.

The challenge of choosing True Leaders

Choosing True Leaders in today's world has become more and more difficult. Our former president and the Republican Party attempted many different strategies to limit voting in the 2020 election, essentially creating fear in the voting public. Vote by mail and fraudulent counts are just two fear strategies. Other separation tactics intend to limit the voting impact of nonwhite voters. These tactics use fear of reprisal against noncitizen family members, leaving citizen family members to do less in the public domain, even voting.

Tactics like this are only used by people who are not True Leaders. Leaders like these only care about themselves, and only some of us, not all of us and each of us. These tactics must be legislatively eliminated from future use by any president or Big Politics by True Leaders.

It's time to look in the mirror and ask ourselves when leading our religious group, our color group, ethnic or gender-based civic group, our sports team, our business unit, or even our family: "Why do we lead one way with these groups and lead or advocate in another way when the issues affect all of us and each of us?" On one side of this controversy are those who lead for the benefit of only the smaller group they interact with daily. On the other side are those who lead with the fundamental thought that we are all human, and we all deserve similar respect and outcomes. In the first case, we often close down the opportunities for some while promoting our select group opportunities. In the second case, opportunities are for all of us and each of us.

Every small group has a similar agenda: to promote its beliefs to gain power and benefits from the rest of us. Most of our leaders are afraid to stand up for all of us and each of us for fear that our own peer group will attack us because of the peer group's fear of losing their benefits.

Until we realize that the solution lies in the fact that we are all connected, we will struggle against time to save ourselves and the planet from our fears of each other. We must begin to learn, and learn quickly, that all of us matter to each other.

We have the power to choose our True Leaders

A True Leader is not a fearmonger who uses separation strategies to pit us against each other. We are all connected to each other. Our True Leaders will understand that, as a world, we are behind the time curve on solving lurking disasters. We know it will take visionary thinking and planning to get ahead of the curve.

To achieve True Leadership, We the People must choose True Leaders.

Chapter 7

We, Too, Can Become True Leaders and Change Lives for the Better

"You don't make progress by standing on the sidelines whimpering and complaining. You make progress by implementing ideas."

— Shirley Chisholm

Sharing our leadership gifts

There are many leaders in our everyday life: our boss/bosses at work, or if we're in school, we think of our teachers/professors. But upon broader thought, after adding "True" to the question, I believe most could think of several others we consider leaders. They could be friends, coworkers, family members, former bosses, or former teachers, to name just a few. We would also suggest people in a broader sphere that includes historical figures like past presidents or others who have changed the world for the better. Consequently, I think we all can agree to a simple fact about our response to True Leadership: "True Leaders changed my life for the better."

Most of us never feel like we will be in a position to be leading anyone, let alone leading for the benefit of all. But even if you have no direct leadership responsibilities for subordinates, constituents, family, or friends, the rest of us still want you to consider us when deciding issues that affect us or when performing your job.

In the big picture, voting is the most obvious example of considering us. However, in day-to-day living, we all interact with each other in many roles as a father, mother, son, daughter, friend, relative, coworker, boss, customer...you get the idea. In all of these interactions, we want you to treat us with respect and provide us with life-enhancing care.

Therefore, we all have an opportunity to be leaders. The question is: Will we be a True Leader, a leader who changes all lives for the better, even if it's in what seems to be very small ways?

Each of us has been given gifts, and common sense tells us that if we each share our particular gift with everyone else and they, in turn, share their gift with us, we all benefit greatly from the collective variety of each of our unique gifts.

Leading by caring with love and understanding

I recently saw a simple example of True Leadership on television with the coach and players of a Little League baseball team that had just lost their final game in the Little League Baseball National Championship round of play. The coach, a True Leader, listened to the players' feelings of disappointment about being less capable than the other team in their descriptions of their loss.

> We all have the opportunity to be a True Leader because of the unique gifts each of us has been given.

Instead of agreeing with their assessment, this True Leader began recounting the teams run to the national championship and how proud he and their parents, in the stands at every game, were of their determination. He said He felt like a second father to each of them. He reminded them that this was not a failure, but a significant life success for all of them and that, thanks to them, he would remember this year forever.

Since we all have the opportunity to be a True Leader, even in small ways, because of the unique gifts each of us has been given, I believe that we should all strive to be True Leaders. The only requirement for True Leadership is caring about all and each of our fellow human beings. In doing so, using our unique gifts, others will recognize us as someone who, just by our presence in their lives, will change their life for the better.

Even if we care about others, striving to be a True Leader will not be easy. We are imperfect. We make judgment errors, and we judge others by our measures. When this happens, we must be kind to ourselves lest we retreat from this greatest of all endeavors. We must realize that, although we have these flaws reflected in mistakes and judging, we also have been given the gift of love and understanding. We must use each of these gifts continuously every day.

Additionally, becoming a True Leader requires observation of our behavior and others' behavior consistently every day. When we observe ourselves interacting with others, we may notice their adverse reaction to our thoughts, comments, and actions. Often, we are not expecting that feedback. When this happens, we realize we have lost connection to the other person.

This has happened to me more than a few times. Lucky for me, while I was writing this book, I had the great fortune to listen to the Arthur Brooks podcast with guest speaker John Gottman while they were talking about contempt. When you observe someone's adverse reaction resulting from your conversation or actions and a subsequent lost connection, it is likely they feel your contempt and perceive your judgment of them. For all of us, contempt is one of the most significant insults we can receive. It says we have negatively judged their intelligence in an attempt to elevate our own. We have just become someone they no longer respect, because none of us likes to be called stupid. It means we may have just lost a friend, or a supporter if you are in a leadership position.

Our judgment comes in many forms: actual negative verbal statements or statement cues, "How can you think that?" Or, "I can't believe you just said that." Or, "Really, you believe that?" Other forms can be just physical: the look on our face, rolling our eyes or a disgusted look and/or a body action such as turning and walking away. We are not perfect, so we will make judging mistakes. As a True Leader, this will set us back many times over our leadership life. This is normal. Do not resort to judgment of yourself. Instead, we must learn from every such experience. By observation and understanding, we will learn to lead in truth and love.

Regaining someone else's trust after a contemptuous judging statement or action is one of the hardest things to do. A true apology is the start of what can be a long road back. You must apologize as soon as you realize the mistake…with no back-peddling. This means that, at this time, you cannot try to explain your thoughts. *Their* thoughts have now become the important part of any immediate discussion. As a True Leader, regaining your friend, relative, or leadership supporter's trust after your mistake in judging is the pinnacle skill of the art of listening for understanding needed to become a True Leader.

Your friend, relative, or leadership supporter did not say or do whatever it was that created the mistake of judgment due to a lack of intelligence. He or she said or acted out of fear. As True Leaders, we must learn to listen to others (not talk) to understand their fears. However, we humans are unlikely to come right out and share verbally why we are afraid. Instead, in our discussions with others, our fears are hidden in both verbal and nonverbal cues. They will be in story form about them or someone else and a description of an event or an encounter that left our sharing person feeling something…angry, sad, dismissed, many possible verbal cues of some kind of hurt.

Oft times, we hear what others are saying, but we miss *why* they are saying it. There can be no understanding of a problem without knowing why it is a problem. To many leaders, *why* may seem irrelevant. If the individual describing a problem does not explicitly articulate why they are concerned, the leader may assume he or she is off the hook for a solution. But that will not solve the problem. We humans often do not clearly articulate the reason for a problem for a variety of reasons: retribution, fear, or embarrassment. As True Leaders, it is our responsibility to calibrate the real "why" to solve the real problem, or more often, by motivating them to solve the real problem. This is not an easy process, but it is essential in the art of listening for understanding and your quest to become a True Leader.

Leading for the benefit of all of us and each of us, not some of us

Why are we accepting leaders at the highest levels of our society who do not follow this simple principle: lead with truth and love by listening for understanding for all of us and each of us? It seems to me that most of them are leading for their benefit, not for all of us. Many would say, "I am leading for the benefit of my stockholders, my company, my constituents, my state, or my something else." But then I must ask: Why are they using the word "my"? It must be because they do not consider all of us, but only some of us, in their leadership decisions. Their connection is to a group smaller than all of us. If these political and business leaders were considering all of us, we would see a much more centrist political system and significantly fewer major business scandals.

They feel justified in their decision/behavior because they satisfy the desire of some group—a state, a religion, a company, an industry, an individual, political party members, stockholders, etc. Leaders at the top level are then allowed to divide us against each other for their benefit, financial, reelection, some special interest, etc.

We all must demand a fair and equitable decision for all, even if we are part of the group that stands to benefit most from something less than fair and equitable for all. Decisions balancing the needs of all are not easy, but not to attempt any balancing just because it's difficult leads to inferior outcomes for most of us.

Big Business favors stockholders, financiers, and executives over all other stakeholders: employees, the community, suppliers, and even customers. Politicians routinely favor Big Business or the wealthy because their reelection campaigns need the money.

The missing ingredients are care and understanding, and the desire to benefit all of us instead of just some of us.

Chapter 8

The Futuristic Sustainability Model

"As we look ahead into the next century, leaders will be those who empower others."

– Bill Gates

Focusing leadership on future sustainability

If we truly are going to change the leadership model to a True Leadership model, many longstanding operating ways of Big Politics and Big Business must change. We do not have time for them to continue to pay lip service to our future. We need change, and we need it now.

Let's take a look at the effects of some leadership styles and behaviors on a sustainable future:

Good	Bad
Futuristically Centrist	Confrontational—win at all cost
Visionary	Vested
Constructive	Destructive
Inclusive	Exclusive or Divisive
All	Some or Me
Lead for Everyone's Benefit	Lead for the Benefit of _____
Nonpartisan	Partisan—only my constituents
Altruistic	Narcissistic
Open/Welcoming	Repressive/Oppressive

Now some fear-separating cost strategies:

Good for Us	Good for Big Business/Big Politics
Then—long-term investment	Now—short-term immediate profit
Cost acknowledgment —sharing	Cost denial—shifting
Resource preservation/restoration	Resource consuming/wasting
Employment enrichment	Employment stagnation
Fair/included	Unfair/separated/excluded
Social security	Only physical security

More fear separating cost-shifting strategies:

Current Generation	Future Generations
Young	Old
Rich	Poor
All	Some
Most Able	Least Able

New leadership solutions for a rapidly changing world

I do not believe that most of our leaders in Big Politics and Big Business are in their jobs only for their ego or the money. I believe most are genuinely trying to make a positive difference for all of us. Unfortunately, they are falling woefully short. They are stuck—*we* are stuck—in a system and process that no longer serves the needs of our future.

We the People must understand the foundational principles for all future top-level leadership and all True Leaders.

True Leaders, whether in Big Politics or Big Business:

- Lead by putting all people above personal wealth, positional gain, or business profit.

- Lead without using fear strategies and tactics to separate people from other people to garner favorable gain in the form of wealth, profits, votes, or legislation.

- Lead by serving all people with fairness and equity when it comes to life's essentials—air, water, food, shelter, safety/security, energy, information/communication, education, and health care.

- Lead from the future, embracing world sustainability without further harm, working to immediately correct current and past abuse of our world, all while building a new economic model based on people rather than profit.

- Lead by partnering to solve the education crisis required for future world development and sustainability.

- Immediately join together with the people of the U.S. and each other and with the other nations of the world to adopt this connecting humanitarian and planetary process.

The model for Futuristic Sustainability

We need a new leadership process model for top-level leadership, and that new model must be Futuristic Sustainability. It's my definition of modeling to be used by Big Politics and Big Business in partnership, where people and the planet are the foundation for the model. It combines the Futuristic Sustainability of people and the planet in long-term planning (30 to 100 years) in continuous and ongoing future transition of society, industry, education, economics, and most significant of all, democracy. As discussed earlier, these are the components of our Life System, and all these components must be connected.

This process crosses the boundary lines of nations, communities, religions, color, ethnicity, gender, business, competition, property, and every other separation line. True Leadership at the top level must understand that sustainability connects everything to everything. No more silo mentality. We, all of us, and each of us, are connected to our world's sustainability.

Futuristic Sustainability is:

The Foundational True Leadership platform (principles)

on which we build the long-term plan/process

connecting everything to each of us and all of us

continuously worked backward, starting with our desired end

to achieve our world's best self and,

the required significant changes to our current Life System of democracy, society, economics, industry, and education.

Changes to Democracy. We are the people, all of us, and each of us, not some of us or few of us. We must re-establish our power over our democracy by electing True Leaders.

Changes to Society. We are equal in our sharing of the basics of life sustenance and opportunity.

Changes to Economics. All people and the planet must drive future investment/return and funding/output equation—not profit.

Changes to Industry. Future creation activities of industry must be linked, planned, prioritized, and completed to sustain our lives and the life of the planet.

Changes to Education. No one is left out of an education that allows each of us to flourish in our best possible life. Nor will any of us be left out of the understanding that we are all responsible for the rest of us.

> We must envision a future world in which all people are treated fairly and equitably no matter who they are, where they live, what they believe, how they look, or any other misconceived separating characteristic.

In our sustainable world of the future, we will no longer be subject to Big Business and Big Industry crashing our economy with its creation of unmanageable bubbles, just to vastly increase the wealth of a few. Nor will we, as taxpayers, have to bail them out after the havoc. Because it operates in a role of support and service, small business is not capable of that type of control of our economics. However, from my experience as a point of reference, small business owners are often the role models for True Leadership. Employees know quickly whether their business leader is a True Leader or not, just by working for him or her. I will discuss later the role of small business in the move to Futuristic Sustainability.

Moving forward, we must envision a future world in which all people are treated fairly and equitably no matter who they are, where they live, what they believe, how they look, or any other misconceived separating characteristic. Additionally, we can no longer use any excuse not to protect the fragile world we live in. Without delay, we must create a process at the top leadership levels of all Big Politics and Big Business organizations and We the People, where these leadership groups are encouraged to dream of what the future will look like 100 years from now. No ideas should be ignored or denigrated. Additionally, these people must meet regularly with their peers from other similar corporate organizations in all industries and all federal government organizations to synthesize and adopt the most probable vision. Once approved, it should be updated with new knowledge continuously. This is not a U.S. process but a free-world process. Delegates from all countries and all industries and businesses should adopt and move toward this future.

Futuristic Sustainability will be a foreign concept to both Big Business and Big Politics. Neither of these institutions has ever operated in the long-term future that We the People are demanding. The future outlook for current Big Business is around three to five years for an average business, ten to thirty years for the current war machine (shrinking every day), and twenty to fifty years for infrastructure and related products. Although Big Politics should operate on a long-term plan, it doesn't, and for the most part, it never has. It works reactively, as evidenced by almost all legislation. It only adopts a change once the political will moves it to do so. We the People can no longer afford the luxury of reactive thinking.

The key to adopting Futuristic Sustainability is the same key that will make it successful: *connection*. Big Business, Big Politics, and We the People are the forward-looking connecting partnership to our future. We can no longer operate in silos. In today's world, it does not work.

In Chapter 10, I discuss China issues and their far-reaching and ever-expanding impact on our global position and the free world's position. We the People of the United States, and the people of the free world, cannot let them dictate the future economic game. The only way we will compete with China now and in the future is to adopt Futuristic Sustainability now. Why? Futuristic Sustainability levels the playing field by connecting our players to the game. If not, we won't even be in the game. China's players are already connected because of their government oversight.

The closest example of this type of process is the climate accord of 2015. However, even that process has fallen woefully short on connecting solutions for global warming. Most countries have not set goals, let alone achievement targets. Once countries set goals and targets, both must be updated regularly, given that knowledge changes significantly every day, with action plans that push for accelerated compliance. The climate accord should not meet intermittently. It should be a permanent world body charged with data collection and significant influence over all countries concerning each country's action plan and progress toward compliance. The largest emitter countries must be linked and eliminate their contribution to the problem simultaneously. They are the wealthiest economies in the world and must be held accountable together.

Additionally, all of the world's nations must work together to assist any country needing help with compliance. During his presidency, Donald Trump removed the United States from the accord. But he is not the only issue. For decades, Big Business has denied global warming.

Finally, I am always including We the People in this new process. Again, global warming is the perfect example of the world's failure to achieve any significant progress on this disastrous planetary and humanity issue. Governments and big businesses have failed us badly on this issue.

We the People of the world must now take control of this life-and-death global warming issue. Science has warned us of the impending danger. They have been too nice. We, all of the world's people, must step in the middle of this cause and demand massive changes, now, in almost everything we currently do and how we do it. Similar to Covid-19, we must demand that our governments and worldwide big businesses immediately change course and work toward a substantial and lasting global warming solution. Just as with Covid-19, we must let the scientists inform us so as to force our big businesses and our governments to accomplish the needed tasks.

An example of the inadequacy of a Big Business global warming solution: solar panels.

I have wanted to put solar panels on my home for more than six years and have tested the market for making the change on several occasions. The price of solar panels has almost doubled over that time frame.

Why the price increase?

A significant portion of the price change comes in the form of a new player in the industry: finance companies. This made it easier for homeowners to buy solar panels and virtually guaranteed that the installers would not go broke. However, this new financing also forced prices up—more players, more perceived risk, more profits for more players.

The government tax credit for solar panels was supposed to lower the price of solar, adding to its adoption prospects. Unfortunately, that government tax credit is the driver of the solar price increase. Once Big Finance entered fully into the business by offering leases of solar systems to homeowners, they raised the installed pricing to pre-tax-credit subsidy rates, basically adding the federal tax credit to the new price of the installed solar panels. The higher price eliminates the financial risks of both installers and financiers. The leasing company has the purchaser sign over their tax credit, which they can use immediately to lessen their tax burden. If the purchaser must pay off the lease early due to a home sale—which is likely—Big Finance just made a fortune. In effect, you lost the tax credit intended to entice you to invest in solar. You now pay the same price you would have paid previously without a tax credit. We customers, taxpayers, and Congress got screwed again by Big Business.

How connections can impact important issues affecting Futuristic Sustainability

The connecting of all top leaders from all industries, governments, and countries should begin to turn the tide of silo decisions to one of encompassing decisions. This is already happening to some extent in solving problems with equity gaps in education, incarceration, safety and security, and housing.

Let's discuss one example involving education.

In Minnesota, where I live, the educational achievement gap between poor children of color and white children is significant. Northside Achievement Zone (NAZ) is an organization working hard to close that gap by looking at all of the factors affecting low academic achievement. As you might expect, several factors affect this achievement gap, none of which are low IQ or lack of motivation. I want to explode whenever I hear people say the achievement gap is due to laziness or lack of basic intelligence. It just isn't true.

NAZ is working with all of the schools in the community it serves—public, charter, parochial—in North Minneapolis. The educators of all of these schools meet regularly to compare notes on new ideas and ideas showing improvement, then implementing them, where applicable, system-wide.

Another issue is combatting absenteeism. To reduce this, parents, teachers, community leaders, volunteers, and NAZ are looking at the reasons children miss school because, as you can imagine, this has a significant impact on performance. The absenteeism of poor children arises from many issues. Volunteers interview parents of children with high rates of absenteeism to determine how that can be corrected. Then volunteers begin providing the needed help to eliminate the cause or causes of the issues.

NAZ has been working on education issues like these for children of color in Minneapolis for the last nine years and is making significant progress toward closing the achievement gap between them and white children of other school districts in Minnesota. They admit to having considerable work left to do but believe they can see the end of this unacceptable situation.

Think about how fast we could solve the educational achievement gap in Minnesota or global warming or anything else if we could only connect Big Politics and Big Business under a banner of *People First*.

Chapter 9

The Institutions of Our Life System

"The next decade cannot be a decade of confrontation and contention. It cannot be East vs. West. It cannot be men vs. women. It cannot be Islam vs. Christianity. That is what the enemies of dialogue want."

— Benazir Bhutto

Our Life System

The world's transition to Futuristic Sustainability must address all components of our Life System:

- Society
- Industry
- Economy
- Education
- Democracy

> Our democratic True Leaders must take back
> control of our democracy from the monetary
> power of Big Business and its benefactors.

We must require our True Leadership to begin building stronger bonds between all five institutions of our Life System by eliminating the following negative roadblocks to connection and replacing them with their positive and empowering counterparts.

Negative		Positive
Some of us and few of us	vs.	All of us and each of us
Fear	vs.	Love and hope
Separation	vs.	Connection
Talking	vs.	Listening
Big Business money in politics	vs.	No Big Business money in politics
Big Business three-stakeholder focus	vs.	Big Business five-stakeholder focus
Profit	vs.	People
Short term	vs.	Long term

To build stronger bonds between our Life System institutions, not only must we define them, but we must also identify their connection weaknesses to the other institutions of our Life System.

Democracy

Our democracy must be the driver for Futuristic Sustainability.

Our democratic True Leaders must take back control of our democracy from the monetary power of Big Business and its benefactors. If they don't, the change we need will not be realized. We the People must find and elect top-level True Leaders that support all of humanity and believe in its goal of Futuristic Sustainability.

Additionally, our democracy and We the People of the United States of America have led the world for the better part of the last two centuries. We must step back onto the leadership mantle and show the free world strong democratic leadership. No more retreating into a nation-state; we must again step up and lead the free world.

Once We the People regain political control, we can begin the process of Futuristic Sustainability. Now the delicate, and yet monumentally necessary, process of connection begins. This is where democracy becomes messy...where massive change gets scary for most of us and where True Leadership becomes critical. Our True Leaders must lead us with love and hope through this battle for unprecedented change, never wavering from the final goal: Futuristic Sustainability.

Several recent issues in the last two decades have resulted in great expense, personal hardship, and loss of lives:

- 9/11 and its aftermath, the Afghan and Iraq wars.
- The 2008 Great Recession.
- The wake-up call to endemic racism
- The Covid-19 pandemic.

All these disasters were foreseen by some but ignored by our leadership at many levels. Let's not continue down this road for one more year. Change needs to start today.

We True Leaders, all of us, like our top-level True Leaders, must help each other with love and hope through this time of significant transition. Our nurturing of each other is far behind the curve of our science, technology, and divisive leadership. We must catch it up rapidly by adopting initiatives and technology that will guarantee Futuristic Sustainability.

> Worldwide democratic politics has evolved into
> *Party politics,* not *people politics.*

The time has come for the elimination of political parties

I know that's a shocking statement, especially in a discussion about democracy, but please bear with me as I make my case.

Democratic politics has evolved into *Party politics,* not *people politics.* It does not matter whether the democracy is a two-party system like the United States or a parliamentary party system like many other democracies. Although We the People vote for our party candidate of choice, the party system rules the outcome of the process.

This has to change, and it can't without abandoning the party concept.

All the party-based systems of government have their deepest roots in money. Even in the earliest democracies, election campaigns required funding for media advertising. Since most candidates were generally unable to fund their campaigns, political parties were created to raise funds for candidates who supported a party's platform. If candidates were willing to abide by the platform, they would be supported financially by the party.

Party politics is driven by money and data. Without it, candidates are severely disadvantaged but also obligated to the party. They must vote the party line on almost all legislation. This is the leading cause of today's divisive politics and the reason for the back-and-forth swing in elections—this election Republicans, next election Democrats. We voters want problems solved while politicians want to win back what they lost the last time.

Party politics is just another example of separation tactics. Democracy is about all of us, and We the People rule. However, for the last two and a half centuries, we have seen politicians win by attacking the character of competing candidates, most of which is truth stretched to its limits, creating confusion and all-out lies, all funded by the party or special-interest political action committees.

There have been many political parties in the history of the United States. Still, most often, it has been the conservative party using attack rhetoric and advertising to gain or retain power. Why? Conservative parties, by definition, are "little, if any, change" parties. They want the status quo to remain. Their fear campaign strategy works because it makes voters feel like their world is about to fall apart. In turn, they fear trying anything new that the other side may be proposing. Conservative politicians have no meaningful solutions to the fear-based attack premise. Their motive is controlling us by getting us to vote them into office.

Lies abound during campaigns, and now lies abound throughout the term. Candidates and the party will say and do anything to win or stay in office. Actual problem-solving legislation rarely occurs because that's not the goal of the party or the candidate. The goal is winning to maintain political party power.

Donald Trump's first presidential election campaign rhetoric made all immigrants into criminals and the Affordable Care Act into the worst health insurance program ever. His fearmongering created his presidency, only to give way to disastrous solutions for children separated from their parents and locked up for months, and federal court case challenges that could leave millions with no health insurance. And these were not the worst of his campaign fearmongering and lies.

Trump's constant use of "I" was a sign of not understanding that it takes all of us to accomplish anything significant. How do we whites solve racism without our Black friends? We don't. How do we solve global warming without China, Russia, Europe, India, and Japan, the other largest emitters? We don't. We have never solved anything significant without others.

Solutions to anything are more manageable with connection than trying to coordinate the separating interests of too many differing groups. Why is it so hard for leadership at the top to understand this?

See Chapter 11 for a more detailed discussion about how and why we should do away with political parties.

Society

Now I will make the connection case between our democracy and our system's other four institutions, moving us to Futuristic Sustainability. The people of the world are all connected, period. As such, we must start to see that we, humanity, have everyday needs for life itself. Without fulfillment of all needs, we humans have little chance of survival, let alone prosperity.

For survival, the psychologist Abraham Maslow developed a list of basic human needs. Maslow's Hierarchy of Needs are as follows:

- Air

- Water

- Food

- Shelter

- Safety/security

- Energy

To that list, I add the following:

- Information/communication

- Education

- Health care

In today's world, without these additional items, we have no way to obtain the knowledge required to secure employment, and without health care, there is no life if you become gravely ill.

Additionally, according to Maslow, safety and security include emotional security, financial security, social stability, and freedom from fear, not just physical security.

To me, the Hierarchy of Needs fits hand-in-hand with the wishes of our country's founders, as expressed in the second paragraph of the Declaration of Independence:

> We hold these truths to be self-evident, that all men are created equal, that they are endowed by their Creator with certain unalienable rights, that among these are life, liberty, and the pursuit of happiness. That to secure these rights, governments are instituted among men, deriving their just powers from the consent of the governed.

Maslow defined the requirements for life, and the Declaration of Independence says that we are all equal. Therefore, I added the other necessary items to keep us equal. Furthermore, the Preamble to the Constitution says:

> We the people of the United States, in order to form a more perfect union, establish justice, insure domestic tranquility, provide for the common defense, promote the general welfare, and secure the blessing of liberty to ourselves and our posterity, do ordain and establish this Constitution of the United States of America.

These two founding documents alone create the foundation for our future, for they put all of us in one all-encompassing group. They define who we are and how we are connected.

Because "society" is all of us people, and we all require the same life-sustaining benefits for survival and prosperity (pursuit of happiness), the Maslow discussion gives us a common way to talk about these life needs and to begin to connect them to the other pieces of our Life System: democracy, industry, education, and our world economy.

I'll repeat my Life Benefit equation for further comments and scrutiny:

> Life Benefit = air, food, water, shelter, safety/security,
> energy, information/communication, education, and
> health care = work/school.

Just by watching the news, we can see from this equation that all of our Life Benefit items are in jeopardy of some type of catastrophe. I won't discuss these potential catastrophic issues here, but please spend a little time thinking about the news reports you have seen in recent years. I'm confident you will have heard negative (life concerning) news reports about each of the Life Benefit items.

Additionally, we have a mismatch in our work/school requirements. Schools are not graduating the workers needed for the 21st century's jobs, let alone the required Futuristic Sustainability jobs. Schools are way behind the accelerated need for well-educated people to fill required positions to prevent future disasters discussed in the first chapter.

The schools are not to blame. You'll find more discussion about education later in the book. For now, let me say that if changes to future schooling are implemented, everyone will be able to obtain a matched, appropriate future job. Accordingly, the equation equal signs indicate that a family unit individual(s) with a job should provide all of the family's Life Benefits.

On the next page, you will see a chart worth reviewing. Based on Maslow's Hierarchy of Needs, I have estimated the percentage of income a family of four—at various income levels—spends on general living expenses. The chart illustrates how much harder it is for a family living in poverty to get by. Values are approximate and are based on the Midwestern U.S. and in U.S. dollars.

My Estimates of the Cost of Living for Various Household Income Levels for a Family of 4
(Values are Approx to Midwest Living)

	Middle Class Twice Poverty		Middle Class 3 Times Poverty		Middle Class 4 Times Poverty		Upper Middle Class	
	%	$	%	$	%	$	%	$
Household Monthly Income		$ 4,300		$ 6,020		$ 8,600		$ 13,760
Income Rate/Hour (combined earners)		$ 25		$ 35		$ 50		$ 80
Annual Income		$ 51,600		$ 72,240		$ 103,200		$ 165,120
My Adjusted Maslow Hierarchy of Needs								
Housing (PMT, Repairs, Maint & RE Tax)	28%	$ 1,204	20%	$ 1,204	14%	$ 1,204	9%	$ 1,204
Food and Household Supplies	22%	$ 946	16%	$ 946	11%	$ 946	7%	$ 946
Util - Gas, Elec, TV, Phone, Internet	8%	$ 344	6%	$ 344	4%	$ 344	3%	$ 344
Health Care (Premiums, Deductibles, etc)	14%	$ 602	10%	$ 602	7%	$ 602	4%	$ 602
Transport (Cars all costs OR Public Trns)	12%	$ 516	9%	$ 516	6%	$ 516	4%	$ 516
Taxes (Incl Soc Sec & Med withholding)	16%	$ 688	11%	$ 688	8%	$ 688	5%	$ 688
Today's Cost of Existence	100%	$ 4,300	71%	$ 4,300	50%	$ 4,300	31%	$ 4,300

Beyond My Adjusted Maslow Calculation

	%	$	%	$	%	$	%	$
Add for New or Upgraded Home	0%	$ -	10%	$ 602	7%	$ 602	12%	$ 1,651
Uitlity add for Home Change	0%	$ -	2%	$ 120	1%	$ 120	2%	$ 275
Add Health Enhance (Braces, Vision, etc.)	0%	$ -	0%	$ -	2%	$ 172	2%	$ 275
Add for Newer Car and/or Extra Car	0%	$ -	0%	$ -	4%	$ 258	4%	$ 550
Add more taxes for Higher Income	0%	$ -	8%	$ 482	15%	$ 1,290	21%	$ 2,890
Savings &/or 401K	0%	$ -	5%	$ 301	10%	$ 860	13%	$ 1,789
Education (Student Loans - Other)	0%	$ -	0%	$ -	5%	$ 430	5%	$ 688
Entertain, Dining Out, Vacation & Other	0%	$ -	4%	$ 241	7%	$ 602	10%	$ 1,376
On the Way to Our Life Dream	0%	$ -	29%	$ 1,746	50%	$ 4,334	69%	$ 9,494
Rounding Difference				$ (26)		$ (34)		$ (34)
Total Income Allocation	100%	$ 4,300	100%	$ 6,020	100%	$ 8,600	100%	$ 13,760

NOTES:
- Official poverty line for a family of 4 is about $25,000 per year annual income
- Middle class has varying definitions. PEW Research Center puts U. S. middle class at $40,000 to $122,000 per year annual income
- Note that at double poverty there is nothing beyond the basic needs
- Currently every family of 4 below double poverty MUST have Government assistance to exist
- Health Care assumes your employer pays for a portion of your care
- Housing assumes PMT is for a Mortgage or Rent
- (combined earners) means if there is more than one earner their hourly wages are combined
- Note that even at almost triple poverty there is barely enough income for an upgraded home, some retirement savings and some entertainment, dining out, or vacation money
- Note that at four times the poverty level we begin to see some real savings, some entertainment, a newer car, some vacation dollars and some ability to retire student debt
- Finally at the upper middle class income level we see a new house, a another car, real retirement savings and real entertainment and vacation dollars

Economy's connection to society and industry

The economy is a system within our Life System. In its purest form, the economy is the commerce transaction system we use to buy/sell goods and services between each other with money—a tool, nothing more, nothing less.

Assumed in the definition of "economy" is *employment*. For all time, we have needed a job to make trades. The job provided the money for us to live. Just a few centuries ago, we were almost all farmers because food, according to Maslow and common sense, was essential to survival. Without today's machines, it took nearly all of us, all of our time, to grow and harvest enough food for survival. Accordingly, in centuries past, the currency was what we grew or killed to eat. Excess food produced was used for trading for the other things we needed: additional food, a house, a cow, a horse, our roof repaired.

Back a few centuries, there was no democracy, so society mostly consisted of an impoverished community coupled with nobility and/or church leadership reaping the benefits of the poor's labor. A century ago in the U.S. and Europe, similar to centuries past without democracy, were a few extremely wealthy businessmen or aristocracy and, for the most part, a poor white population coupled with an impoverished Black population. Other nonwhite races were treated as lower class and generally fell into a significantly inferior economic status, even if they were citizens.

When democracy progressed past World War I, the equity split between rich and poor was significant, especially for people of color. For much of the 20th century, the United States could boast the largest middle class in the world—as long as you didn't consider people of color. For those few decades in the 20th century, union wages and benefits helped close the income gap between rich and poor, but recently, it has widened and is continuing to extend.

Significantly different from a few centuries ago, our current national and world economy is diverse, allowing employment in very tiny sectors of the gigantic world Economy. Accordingly, in today's diverse society, our economic system is far more complicated. We have many industries, some of which did not exist ten years ago, not to mention those that did not exist a century ago. We have services to repair the many products we own. We have multiple ways to fund transactions: credit cards, debit cards, checking accounts, mortgages, stocks, bonds, notes…no longer just cash and loans. We have many countries with different currencies, making trade between countries even more complicated.

Still, today's job in our tiny sector of the world economy must provide money for everything we need to live. However, for many of us—again, often minority people of color or recent immigrants—today's version of Maslow's Needs is not covered by the income from a job. People in this category are living on the edge of disaster every day. Many people of color, recent immigrants, and even lower-end middle-class whites who typically have a comfortable but not extravagant life could not weather the economic effects of the 2008 recession or Covid-19. Many lost their homes, their savings, their retirement, and their sense of job security. Middle-class whites have had enough income and savings to cover not only Maslow's Needs but some luxury items: a bigger house, a car, a vacation, more clothes, dining out, and entertainment. But even this group of us has lost ground in wealth over the last several decades as wealth has moved significantly to the top 1% of us. We are leaving even our upper-middle-class far below its relative place of twenty to thirty years ago.

Our democracy has now existed for coming up on 250 years. Per our founding documents, the equity between all of us and each of us should be reflected in our lives, meaning that our job and our job security should be enough to cover, at a minimum, Maslow's lowest tiers of needs.

Economic pressures emphasize short-term goals

Our economy, and frankly most of the world's economy, functions as a quasi-free market system. The free market slogan and simple definition are: whatever the market will bear, i.e., the highest price people will pay for a product or service. When people stop buying at the highest price, the price will start ratcheting downward until it settles at a price where people start buying again.

Market pressure, in effect, controls prices. An equally important corollary is: if demand is high and the supply is low, the price will continue to rise. I added the word *quasi* to the front of "free market" because governments often set commerce regulations and regulatory prices for specific products. Drugs are often in this category. Also, single-source sellers will set a price very high because they can. Drugs, again, are common for this type of pricing.

For Big Business, this free market economy generally operates on a common stock ownership basis, meaning the profit rewards go to the owners of the stock by virtue of stock price increases. The stock price goes up presumably because the company's value increases when it makes more money, though many other factors increase the stock price. Investor speculation has a significant impact on stock prices too. Suppose investors believe the company will continue to make money (future profits). In that case, the stock market will adjust stock prices upward for that belief and downward for confidence in the opposite future outcome (losses).

Generally, company stock is bought and sold on one of the U.S. stock exchanges. The New York Stock Exchange (NYSE) is by far the largest in the world. The National Association of Security Dealers Automated Quotations (NASDAQ) is another well-known U.S. stock exchange. Stocks listed on market exchanges can be purchased and sold by virtually anyone with money. For any company stock, prices rise and fall in correlation to the buying/selling transaction prices investors complete in company stock.

Earlier, I discussed that Big Business often uses tax relief and low-cost debt to buy back its stock. Since this maneuver doesn't change the company's overall value, it means that fewer outstanding shares will result in a higher per-share value. Who does this benefit? Company management and shareholders.

If the company's equity increases, generally, the stock price will increase. In the purest sense, you can calculate stock price by dividing equity by the number of outstanding shares of stock.

In Big Business, stock price considerations rule because it affects the executive team compensation, including bonuses for stock price increases. Corporate executive bonuses are often in stock options, giving the executives incentives to make decisions around increasing the company's stock price, such as stock buybacks—no real increase in company value, but an increase in stock price.

> Our current stock price decision-making process focuses on short-term goals and kills innovation.

That's why today's Big Business executive team members make only those decisions that will positively impact the stock price in the relatively short-term, significantly less than even the low end of my 30 to 100 year long-term Futuristic Sustainability time frame. In fact, in almost all cases, these short-term manipulations are designed to maintain a relatively stable but ever-increasing stock price over less than five years—the typical tenure of Big Business senior executives. Why?

This focus on stock price sets short-term decision-making as the primary driver of Big Business decisions, profit over people. Until we scrap Big Business's short-term decision-making (less than five years) and replace it with long-term decision-making (30 to 100 years), we will be unable to make the change to Futuristic Sustainability.

Remember, one of our top-level foundational True Leadership elements was to put people over profits, not the reverse.

Our current free-market capitalistic world economy has increased the standard of living for many over the last fifty years. However, that growth has been sporadic, spotty, and very susceptible to recession and deterioration in many sectors. Our current political climate is a direct result of that deterioration in rural America and the ups and downs of emerging democracies. We need the stability of Futuristic

Sustainability to create an economic system at the top, our largest companies that drive economic transition over time, not an economic system that picks winners and losers based only on current stock price and short-term profit.

And there are losers in this short-sighted focus on stock value and profits. Why are Sears, J. C. Penney, K-Mart, and other retail giants gone or on the way out? Why is General Electric struggling? Why didn't the original AT&T invent the cell phone? Why didn't one of the railroads create FedEx or UPS? Why didn't Sears or J. C. Penney create Amazon? After all of GE's acquisitions under Jack Welch, why are they now consolidating?

Similar to GE and Jack Welch are all of our largest tech companies. Microsoft, Apple, Google, and Facebook have acquired many smaller companies over their growth years—stock price increase years. Why? They claim they are buying needed technology to enhance their ability to provide a better customer experience. I say they are buying these companies to limit future competition and future innovation by the smaller companies that may interfere with their stable stock price, just like Jack Welch and GE.

In my opinion, the primary reason for all of these corporate giants' failures to innovate is the stock market. Once the companies become established and have stable earnings, it's virtually impossible to innovate, even though they generally have a treasure trove of talented people. The current stock market does not allow the risk. This must change for the betterment of all of us. But it cannot, while under the umbrella of our current stock price decision process. Real innovation cannot and should not be relegated to only startup companies.

Required changes to the Big Business decision-making process

We the People must take steps to change Big Business leadership to True Leadership. Changing the focus of Big Business from short-term decision-making to long-term decision-making will likely take longer than changing Big Politics. In fact, in my mind, this is likely to be the most difficult—but also the most crucial—part of reaching our goal of Futuristic Sustainability.

Big Business must hold itself responsible by recommending federal laws that significantly tie its hands on profit over people. We must take away the stock price element in Big Business decision-making and Big Business's financial influence on Big Politics.

Before dealing with the stock price element, Big Business must recommend to Congress that any company or business association or any other variation of business-supported groups be barred from lobbying or campaign funding Congress or the president, period, for any purpose. Big Business is not a people; they should not have the political power they now have.

To take away the stock price element in Big Business decision-making, Big Business must recommend to Congress that any leadership position in the top three business management levels be paid only on a fixed cash value basis. In other words, "No short-term incentives, period." No bonus profit motives, no stock options, etc. Bonuses can be offered and paid based only on long-term achievement (beginning at five years), targets of long-term goals (beginning at ten years), and maintaining the entity's equity parameters.

There can also be no long-term financing of stock buybacks. Long-term borrowing and excess cash are for growth investment capital for new product development and required employment growth.

I hope that the current top leaders in Big Business realize they are causing the lion share of the chaos in our democracy and our world economy. Then with safety in numbers, the top 100 U.S. Big Business CEO's will get together and agree to adopt what I have just proposed. My hope would be that these Big Business True Leaders will be the ambassadors to the rest of the Big Business community, the stockholder community, and Congress in advocating for these legal changes by leading their peers to do the right thing, and that this process will spread to the other big businesses located in other countries.

We must also legislatively change the status of big businesses that provide societal needs to nonprofit status, removing any connection to an extended profit. Societal-needs big businesses are those that fall under my adjusted Maslow Hierarchy of Needs listing. Generally, any big business that provides products or services to sustain our life—anything to do with air, food, water, shelter, safety/security, energy, information/communication, education, and health care. I would also encourage regular big businesses to apply for nonprofit status for the reason discussed below.

Societal-needs big businesses would be funded with fixed value preferred stock, providing needed equity capital for the company and everlasting fixed dividends to investors. Unlike common stock, this preferred stock would be a no-market stock, meaning that it would not be allowed to be bought and sold on any stock exchange after its initial offering. With no market, the stock would not fluctuate in value, eliminating its focus on stock value. The preferred stock and long-term debt would fund long-term project-based solutions to society problems. However, as nonprofits, they would not pay income taxes. None of these businesses would be allowed any ties to for-profit entities. This is explained in more detail in Chapter 12.

Executive True Leaders in this business sector will be compensated with salaries and fixed bonuses on the achievement of timetables, progress benchmarks on the way to a final implemented solution to a society problem, and the maintenance of their equity within parameters established by their long-term plan. Leadership's focus moves entirely to long-term people-based solutions with no stock market connections of any kind.

Who are not societal needs big businesses? Generally, luxury item businesses, small businesses, dining, travel, and entertainment businesses. Most businesses in the United States are in these categories. Luxury item businesses are any business that creates or sells high-value products that we don't necessarily need to live but want: a big house, an expensive car, jewelry, almost any kind of television or electronics that is not required communication and/or information (in today's world, a phone and/or computer is required), and the list goes on.

Even if the big business is not a societal-needs big business, they must also begin to work together with Big Politics to set long-term goals for their industry. Many can go a long way to help in the facilitation of the transition of societal-needs change projects. Leadership attempts to circumvent the intent of these changes would be met with criminal penalties.

> If we are to meet the needs of the new economy, we need more well-educated workers.

Education: the key to Futuristic Sustainability

Now let's talk about the education crisis in the United States.

If we are to meet the needs of the new economy, we need more well-educated workers. Big Business is sitting on the sidelines, waiting for Big Politics to solve this problem. Big Business, again, believes this is not its problem for a couple of reasons. One, it has always been a government issue. Two, most big businesses are multinational corporations and know they can get needed labor cheaper in other countries, often U.S. educated workers who moved back home.

The education crisis is a "money and will" problem. Big Business needs more people for its expanded role in Futuristic Sustainability. Therefore, it needs to help pay for the education and/or training of the people it needs. This has become a necessary business expense, but one that is not yet in process. Suppose we are going to avoid, limit, or eliminate catastrophic disasters and other substantial world issues. In that case, we will need researchers and technicians and degreed and advanced-degreed employees in all industries like never before.

But this is not just an advanced degree or training issue. It is a preschool, grade school, and high school issue too. Big Business needs to step up in conjunction with Big Politics and begin contributing to public schools in the more impoverished communities of the wider area in which they reside and serve, including declining rural areas created by poor economic decisions of the past. They must work together with parents, teachers, education experts, and community leaders on ideas and best practices for all aspects of the education process, including the *Why* of lower attendance rates of children of color, poor children, and non-English speaking children. You can't learn if you are not there.

We must erase this educational outcome difference in our children's current generation, whether urban or rural children. There are only two reasons we can't, and they are money and the will of Big Business: the same group that needs them the most.

Finally, Big Business must connect with Big Education, Big Government, and We the People to create the resources needed to fulfill the required future jobs. Big Business itself, not a separate industry, must become an education resource, no longer only an education user. They do not need to provide advanced education. Still, they need to develop technical training of significant numbers of their required workforce in conjunction with existing and new educational institutions.

In summary

- Societal needs are for all of us and each of us.

- Many of the societal needs revolve around home.

- Many of us are well below what is required to gain anything remotely close to the pursuit of happiness.

- Many of the required changes need substantial new jobs and training.

- We must cut out excessive profit of those economic needs, and accordingly we need a new business model that focuses on solutions, not profit.

The question many will be asking is: How do we pay for this? Read on. I'll cover this in the next chapter.

Chapter 10

Connecting Big Politics, Big Business, and We the People for Futuristic Sustainability

"Real change, enduring change, happens one step at a time."

– Ruth Bader Ginsburg

The first step in building our vision of the next 100 years

Once the recommended limiting legislation is passed by Congress and signed by the president, we all—Big Business, Big Politics, and We the People—can begin the work of creating the process I discussed earlier. The linking of groups of visionary True Leaders from Big Business, Big Politics, and We the People must forecast the future of 100 years from now. It must be the world we envision for our grandchildren and great-grandchildren. From this vision, the combined group of True Leaders will begin to develop the tools we need to create the future.

In 100 years, what will our economy look like? What will our education system look like? What will business and industry look like? What will our society look like?

We need process tools to link these subsystems to each other to create our new world system to achieve our 100-year future. The last primary linking requirement is to begin to develop both the smaller process systems within each subsystem and, finally, the products required for the transition to our 100-year future.

> What happens when the profit motive trumps every other consideration in decision-making for Big Business?

Big Business is focused on making a profit. In their context, employment has only to do with the fewest people necessary to do the production job. The "production job," as I am using it here, is the whole group of employees needed at their company, from the CEO to the line workers or programmers, or whoever produces the final product.

There are substantial numbers of missing employees when the goal is only profit. Eliminating the profit-only goal will create the need for employees that optimize production for less waste, longer life, reuse, reengineering of older products, exploring future product needs, forecasting and resolving negative issues of their products on the environment, exploring new ideas and solutions far from their current product line, and many others. It literally opens the door to many other opportunities for increased revenue and employment in and out of their contemporary realm of products. The cost of these new employees will be appropriately placed in its current operating statement, as well as amortized over the future benefits of the products on the planet, rather than charging future generations to repair or replace short-lived products and planetary cleanup.

Let me give you an example from my experience of when the profit motive trumps everything else.

Not long ago, my refrigerator's main control board died after fifteen years of flawless operation. The refrigerator still looked great and would've continued to serve our needs, but I couldn't get a new control board. I had to buy a new refrigerator. What a waste of resources!

This is an example of changes to Big Business's operating processes we so desperately need. Eliminating the profit-only mentality from the equation would help save the planet by giving us a choice in our buying decisions: fix or replace something missing for a long time.

Here's another employment issue. Our most profitable large companies employ a significant number of their production workers as contractors, not employees. This allows them to avoid paying benefits such as health care, vacation, and retirement available to actual employees. Sidestepping employment law is today's version of the 19th century's employment practices, the power of Big Business and Big Politics over lowly workers. And the sad truth is that these workers often feel that they have no choice but to accept whatever job is given to them. As these workers age, they'll be left with no retirement accounts, and their hope for opportunities such as promotion within the company is usually nonexistent. But if they need a paycheck and can't find it elsewhere, what choice do they have but accept contract work? When faced with either a bad choice or no choice at all, there's only one option.

Imagine the jobs once we begin to have a shared vision and long-term plan based on humanity and the world. Instead of the current silo mentality, in which every government and every big business operates for its own best interest, we could have a world in which:

- They and we work for all of us and each of us, and the health of our planet.

- All of us have enough to eat every day of every year.

- The water we drink is so clean we can dip a glass into almost any pool for a quenching sip.

- The air is so clean we go outside for some refreshing, deep breaths.

- What we need is produced in the best place for its use or consumption, always considering the overall effects on our planet.

- We use the most updated processing for production, wasting little, harming nothing, and recycling everything possible.

- All of us and each of us have had an education second to none, preparing us for the work of our dreams.

- The worries of sickness are slipping away as we conquer disease.

- Conflict between people has not occurred since the start of our Futuristic Sustainability strategy because everyone has a life worth living in their pursuit of happiness.

> Big Politics and Big Business have excluded us
> from the major decisions affecting the direction
> of our country and the democracies of the world.
> Now, We the People must demand a seat at
> the table.

Adding citizen delegates to connected industry groups

What I described in the previous section sounds like utopia, but it can be the reality if only we decide this is what We the People want, and we take action to demand this from our top leaders in Big Politics and Big Business.

Big Politics and Big Business have excluded us from the significant decisions affecting our country's direction and the world's democracies. Now, We the People must demand a seat at the table to ensure that this exclusion never happens again.

We must become, along with delegates from Big Business and Big Politics, a delegate-recommending group providing and ensuring that the focus of legislation and world direction is truly on all of us and each of us. Citizen-industry group members would take an oath that they represent We the People only, replacing the no-longer-needed Big Business lobbyists. Oath violations would be grounds for immediate dismissal. Big businesses must now replace lobbyists with actual senior executives with decision-making power to represent them at industry group meetings.

There will be many groups from Big Politics/Big Government and Big Business, and therefore, there will be many citizen groups representing us, We the People. Groups are not based on product produced but by service category.

There will be eight industry headline groups loosely following Maslow's Hierarchy: energy, food and water, health and welfare, education/communication/information, resource management, transportation and logistics, safety and security, support tools: funding and finance.

For example, under the industry headline group of health and welfare, health care would include all health care industries involved in health: insurance, pharmaceuticals, providers—hospitals, doctors, health clinics, etc. Also, in that headline group would be the welfare industry members comprised of industries involved in housing, food and water, energy, education, etc., safety and security, and finally support tools—funding and financing. As you can see, health and welfare has needed crossover from other headline groups.

Each industry headline group will have a delegate count match of each state's congressional members to be chosen by each state's senators and/or governors based upon general business and some relevant knowledge of the group's mandate and little, if any, ties to the Big Business group.

Such individuals' compensation shall be 80% of the congressional salary schedule with a travel and housing allowance. Positions should be limited to two six-year terms, and no member will be allowed to move to any company within the specific industry group represented after holding this position. Initial representative appointment terms will be staggered by two-year increments with no representative serving more than eighteen years. Senate and House staff members assigned to particular groups should be limited but are charged with presenting the congressional members' thoughts.

Within industry groups, multiple committees will be working on many issues and recommendations to the overall industry group and headline group for final recommendation to the connecting group. All headline groups will have horizontal links to each other since they are all connected in some form or another. Other horizontal and vertical solution partner collaborating organizations such as nonprofits, government agencies, and foundations will be sought out for connection concepts and solutions.

Roll-up delegates of specific industry groups shall be four representatives from each of the Big Business groups and the people group elected by their peers to represent their group at the connecting group meetings. As in the lower group, Senate and House staff members will be assigned by the congressional representative. These connecting groups' primary goal is for business and the people to recommend required legislative action to implement necessary steps to carry out the Futuristic Sustainability plan. However, I expect that there will be several connecting group meetings before recommendations are passed to the legislators.

Another two levels of connecting groups extend up to the free-world countries, integrating the process to all countries and down to states, counties, and cities. All governing bodies must be integrating and executing similar solutions to the world's most significant issues.

The recommendations that I am talking about are comprehensive, like never before. The plan pieces must be linked to responsibilities for Big Business, Big Government/Big Politics, and international players of Big Business and Big Government/Big Politics, if required, which will occur frequently. Responsibilities include who does what, what's the timetable, how this is funded, etc. Input from many outside organizations in business and government will often be needed to get required information.

This process for meeting and executing must include review, updates, revisions, and re-executions.

At all sets of group meetings, there will be times where a concluding solution is not attainable at that time. A concluding solution is not required, but movement *toward* a concluding solution is required. We are looking 100 years into the future. We must have an idea where we are going, but it is unrealistic to think we can get there today. It is also unrealistic to make no progress toward a solution soon. Big Business and we must make appropriate small-step recommendations to achieve the final goal. Big Business and Big Politics must then implement anything necessary to achieve the next steps toward the ultimate goal.

Futuristic Sustainability goals and strategies will solve the problem

Let's pause for a moment and discuss the difference between goals and strategies. A goal is an ultimate solution to or movement toward an ultimate solution. A strategy is the mechanics of how we achieve the goal.

In our current Big Politics, the strategy is where the breakdown occurs. Generally, the Democrats want the government to solve the problem, costing us individual taxpayers more in taxes. The Republicans want the individual to solve his/her own problem, costing no direct tax dollars but plenty of indirect tax dollars or added out-of-pocket cost—and maybe even lives.

What do I mean by indirect tax dollars or added costs? Here are two examples:

- If the child of a low-income family with no medical insurance falls ill, the parents often have no choice but to take the child to the nearest hospital's emergency room. That visit may cost thousands of dollars, but the hospital has to write it off since the parents can't pay. Who ends up paying? The rest of us. The hospital is not going to lose money. It can predict with much certainty how often this will occur, meaning the rest of us just pay more every time we go to the hospital. Over time those extras keep getting larger because of the hospital's profit motive.

- If a young person has no hope for a good job because of the cost of training or college education, he or she will be vulnerable to the call of drug addiction and criminal behavior. Who pays for his or her prosecution, incarceration, or therapy? You guessed it. And sometimes the cost is someone's life. In contrast, if this young person could get the education or training that would allow him or her to have a happy, productive life, that person would be working and paying taxes instead of adding to the public burden.

On the national defense question, generally, the sides are reversed, with the Republicans typically enthusiastic about spending plenty of our tax dollars on the military. Unfortunately, too often, we're spending our military dollars on last century's technology. With technology changing the way wars are fought, let's make sure we spend our money on "the right stuff."

> What you won't see in a futuristic sustainable world is death and destruction and unbridled costs and deficits attributed to unforeseen catastrophes.

A new economic model for sustained growth

Now let's talk about how to pay for all this.

The simple answer is: we'll pay for it with the jobs created once we begin to have a common vision and long-term plan based on humanity and the world. Opportunity always creates work. Opportunity to make our world a better place for all of us and each of us creates work for all of us and each of us. The real question then is: How do we create an economic system that pays for the work?

The current system rewards only those who can afford to invest in its potential outcome. That won't work for all of us and each of us. Therefore, we must create a new economic model in which the rewards go to everyone. It's within our reach if we have the will.

Creating a new economic model is one of the first Big things we must change. Lucky for us, we do not need to change it significantly. And the required change is tied fundamentally to the long-term nature of Futuristic Sustainability.

The new economic model will move us away from the short-term stock price and profit economic model (discussed in an earlier chapter) to a sustained-growth model. Investment funding will be based on the continuous and sustained development of people-based systems that drive our world's growth. Instead of the short-term stock price investment mentality, money will flow to these all-encompassing growth strategies driven by a long-term, well-stated plan tied to a connected economy. Why? Because risk is diminished. Strategic plans of this type connect all industries and raise all returns because it lowers risk for everyone.

We have seen this before in the war economy of World War II. However, in the war example, sooner or later, the war ends and the accelerated economy slows down. In our case, it's not a war but the continuing self-induced direction of Futuristic Sustainability.

The link between Big Politics and Big Business, with We the People as moderators, will give Big Business something it has tried to develop but is incapable of doing because it has only one weapon: price—or, in some cases, a monopoly. The link gives Big Business the absolute world of people as customers. Done connectedly, opportunities are less risky—the result is an ability to fund much larger endeavors because of the lower risk.

Closing the loop on this discussion is the ability to hire people from around the world. Unlike today, under Futuristic Sustainability we will begin to bring the standard of living up for all of us and each of us.

Under the new economy, investment capital will come in the form of preferred stock with guaranteed dividends and an original price (no market price, since it isn't traded on any stock exchange) and long-term debt. Both dividends and interest will be deductible as a business expense for taxes. In addition to investment capital provided by the preferred stock and the long-term debt, future accumulated earnings, no longer required to increase stock price, can be utilized for future investments while maintaining an equity cushion against short-term losses.

I also see much more global government funding of societal-needs big businesses. The World Bank does some of this type of funding, but now we must move toward a World Bank concept on steroids. An initial international project must redefine and reorganize our free-world banking system, tying it directly to Futuristic Sustainability.

Finally, if you're reading between the lines, you can see a minimum gradual increase in prices and taxes. However, what you won't see in a futuristic sustainable world is death and destruction and runaway costs and deficits attributed to unforeseen catastrophes. You won't see bailouts of Big Business, significant stopgap financial assistance programs because of the poverty of massive portions of the population, and record-breaking costs of delayed solutions piling on the future generations of our country and the world.

Corruption's impact on the prospects for Futuristic Sustainability

The partnership between Big Politics and Big Business must work tirelessly on ending corruption while beginning to bring the poorest people of the world up little by little to a new standard of living. Big Business, once it adopts its new role, can be the missing piece to many of these problems. Instead of giving untrained—sometimes corrupt—politicians funds to solve poverty and business startups (economic development), Big Business can assist in both, while Big Politics helps with corruption and democracy issues. Based on experience, the answer seems to be long-term versus short-term solutions with our hands on the purse strings and a real Big Politics and Big Business partnership.

The China economic power example

On my list of potential disasters from Chapter 1 is China's rise as an economic power. China's rise is not actually the disaster; the disaster is our Big Politics and Big Business way of dealing with it.

My theory of China's long-term plan—colonize the developing world to steal their resources (oil, minerals, crops, water, etc.) is all to be carried out, in their mind and their propaganda, on the up and up. Let's take a look at how it works.

1. Loan African, Asian, and South American countries Big money to develop infrastructure that is supposed to help the developing countries create jobs and build wealth for the targeted country. However:

    i. China begins by bribing public officials to get the proposal approved quickly.

    ii. China builds the infrastructure to its standards with its companies with no senior-level team members, higher-level labor jobs, or input from the developing country—roads, bridges, railroads, ports, airports, and power plants/grids.

    iii. China builds permanent housing for the Chinese workforce forcibly secured from the developing country's citizens.

    iv. China controls the operation of all infrastructure created and uses Chinese employees to manage and operate it.

2. Call in the loans once the developing country cannot pay the debt.

    i. Obviously, with no significant new jobs for developing country employees, there is little increase in tax revenue to retire the debt.

    ii. Under the loan agreement's default loan clause, the developing country must transfer the collateral to China (built infrastructure and country resources) to a specified Chinese business, which now has complete control of everything China wanted.

3. China's permanent housing camps now provide bases from which to protect its workers and its newly acquired assets and give a needed excuse to place military troops worldwide.

It sounds eerily familiar. We in the U.S. did this through our free market system, in which private companies put in the investment to exploit resources from developing countries and corruptible politicians. Many of our corporate deals have since fallen apart due to corrupt government takeovers and lack of needed real investment in the impoverished country.

China's probably won't fall apart—at least for a while—because I am forecasting their military involvement in the final deal.

> We are losing the battle with China because
> of our single-minded focus on an unregulated
> free market system and our refusal to hold
> our democratic governments and our largest
> businesses—even our own government and
> businesses—to the highest standards of
> non-corruption.

I speculate on this whole story to illustrate my point:

1) If the original corporate resource deals had been done as a true partnership between two democratic countries to create jobs and build wealth for the people of the developing country, the outcome would have been different.

2) If we, as a democratic country, helped significantly build the wealth of the country and its citizens while educating and policing the growth of their democracy, we will get a better outcome and a true democratic non-corrupt ally.

3) Truly building infrastructure and the groundwork for a significant middle-class wage base for the locals—as we did with Japan and Europe after World War II, and South Korea after the Korean War—will guarantee much better success...

In the long-term, China will fail, as we did, unless they devote substantial military resources or make the deal into a real partnership by developing the whole country. At this time, it appears that they, like us, are trying the shortcut, which won't work.

We in the U.S. and the rest of the developed world have the same opportunity as China if we choose—and we *should* choose—to make a real deal with the developing world now. Democracy is much better than authoritarian governments and dictatorships for people of the U.S. and the world. Still, we are currently losing the battle with China because of our single-minded focus on an unregulated, completely free market system and our refusal to hold our democratic governments and our largest businesses—even our own government and businesses—to the highest standards of non-corruption.

The concept of Futuristic Sustainability should be our weapon against China's foray into the undeveloped world. China's initial step was infrastructure. Now it's technology, especially its authoritarian surveillance technology. Undeveloped governments will now easily spy on their citizens and make it much harder for us to bring them to democracy, not to mention China's ability to influence and control other countries' populations.

China uses its authoritarian way of competing with the United States in that it automatically connects everything to its interest. Our unconnected business and politics have been losing this battle for years. We will continue to lose the fight until we are no longer a viable competitor unless we connect our Big Politics and Big Business to humanity in our fight for the freedom of the world's people.

My goal for Futuristic Sustainability

I am not arrogant enough to believe that every idea I have outlined will be adopted. Still, most of the plans' overall objective must be achieved to prevent a return to the same old Big Politics and Big Business cozy bedfellows' way of operating. And I believe we are on a short timetable before significant negative consequences of my list of disasters will change life forever for the world's population.

Finally, and most importantly, none of the ideas I have presented will work if the leadership of Big Business and Big Politics looks the other way and continues with business as usual. We the People are the only ones who can force their hand. Together we can elect new True Leaders, or they can get on board, the first step in changing our future. I'm hoping for the latter, just as I'm hoping Big Business chooses to get on board by recommending the needed legislative changes to their way of operating.

A plan always starts with a goal. Because our common humanity links us together, we will have multiple goals, not just one. Let's make a list of our plan's very broadest goals, keeping in mind our foundational premise: the world is for all of us and each of us. Accordingly, we all deserve life, liberty, and the pursuit of happiness—the American Dream extended to the world.

My abbreviated picture of Futuristic Sustainability 100 years from now

All eight billion people have:

- At least all of Maslow's lowest two tiers of their needs met.

- A balance of work and leisure that satisfies (the pursuit of happiness).

- The planet's climate is back in balance.

- Resources are being preserved and protected for sharing with future generations.

- Air, water, and food are free from harm and sufficient for us people and the other species of the world.

- Big Politics, Big Business, and We the People continue working together:

    ◦ To provide meaningful work and leisure for people of the world.

    ◦ To provide safety and security for all people against everyday issues and cataclysmic disasters.

    ◦ To create the tools needed for life.

Part III

We All Must Lead...Now!

Chapter 11

Big Politics Leaders Must Become True Leaders ...and Lead Now!

"Ask not what your country can do for you; ask what you can do for your country."

— John F. Kennedy

A call to action

Democracy is not so much about majority rule, but about *people* rule because the country, and the world, is all of us, not *some* of us. Instead, we've created a more fruitful life for some...but for fewer and fewer over time, relatively speaking.

Unfortunately, we have not moved far toward the ideals and responsibility President John F. Kennedy laid on all of us. In the sixty years since his inaugural address, many of the significant human issues he raised have not only not been eliminated but, in most cases, are significantly worse.

We are failing to achieve movement on "Ask what you can do for your country" or the world because we missed the connection he made earlier in the address:

Now the trumpet summons us again, not as a call to arms, though arms we need, not a call to battle, though embattled we are, but a call to bear the burden of a long twilight struggle, year in and year out, rejoicing in hope, patient in tribulation, a struggle against the common enemies of man: tyranny, poverty, disease and war itself.

Can we forge against these enemies a grand and global alliance, North, South, East and West, that can assure a more fruitful life for all mankind? Will you join in that historic effort?

Unfortunately, We the People never joined the effort to create a more fruitful life for all mankind. Instead, we created a more fruitful life for some, but for fewer and fewer over time. We can no longer ignore President Kennedy's call to action against those same—and some new, common, but even more powerful—enemies of man: tyranny, poverty, disease, and now global warming, and finally, still, war itself.

We the People must demand moral and ethical True Leadership

We are all human and all citizens of the world living in a fragile environment in which hope, not fear, must motivate us to create and maintain governments that continuously strive to act on behalf of each of us and all of us to promote and achieve an improving and lasting world.

> Our sustainable world is slipping away. Many
> of our life-sustaining resources are unprotected
> and being squandered for the benefit of
> only a few. Even our everyday safety is now
> becoming questionable.

We are all connected and one with each other, and therefore we all must have respect for each other. Although we are one, we are also not all the same, and as such, we must demand that our world governments promote the dignity of each of us and all of us by affording each of us and all of us an opportunity to become and maintain the best we can be.

Our world has become more and more fragile and tenuous. Our lives have become less and less under our control and more under the control of someone else. Our sustainable world is slipping away. Many of our life-sustaining resources are unprotected and being squandered for the benefit of only a few. Even our everyday safety is now becoming questionable.

We, along with our governments and True Leaders, must create a hope-based world economy in which opportunity, wealth, and sustainability are shared with each of us and all of us. Hope cannot be based on money but must be based on sustainability of opportunity and sustainability of resources. If hope is based only on wealth, we will continue to see prosperity going to the few.

We must demand our world governments protect each of us and all of us from the tyranny of the few. We must require our political and business leaders to be true to us, not to themselves. True Leadership in Big Politics and Big Business must now work together with us to create a better and safer world for all of us, not for only a few of us. In other words, we need moral and ethical leaders.

Moral and Ethical True Leadership:

- Eliminates the money for the favorable treatment connection between Big Politics and Big Business.

- Seeks partnerships between business, government, and other industry leaders to generate new concepts to solve all of humanity's problems by focusing on people not profit.

- Creates a vision that outlines the future direction of their industry or organization and embraces the required visionary long-term plans that realistically avoids predictable future costs and/or catastrophes (30+ year plans, not short-term stopgap measures) for all generations to come.

- Creates equivalent benefits and opportunities for all of us and each of us, not some of us or few of us.

- Accrues all costs—both current and future costs—no longer pushing current costs on to future generations, whether through future taxes or future higher prices.

Moral and Ethical True Leadership in Big Business:

- Realizes and accepts that an advanced-educated society is in their best interest and, therefore, must contribute immediately and significantly to meet their interests; otherwise, their available workforce and their available customer base will diminish, undermining their continuing existence.

- Allows people to decline personal information sharing or capturing while retaining all access to necessary universal information securing tools and data.

We must demand that our political leaders support us in rebuilding and expanding the middle class

We must build strong and lasting public/private industry partnerships, including We the People, based on accountable and measurable social and fiscal responsibility in which human and planetary resources are fully accounted for in the following societal-impacted industries:

- Energy research, production, distribution, and safety.

- Food/water research, production, distribution, and safety.

- Health (medical) and welfare (food, energy and housing) systems.

- Space exploration and Earth preservation planning and execution.

- Secure technology integration into all of the above.

We must change our laws to promote the above behavior from our largest businesses.

We must build a new education system funded by a public and private partnership to meet the goal of rebuilding and expanding the U.S. middle class as well as eliminate the education opportunity divide. When successful, we will fundamentally change the lives of the disenfranchised, who will no longer be seeking crime or terrorism—often the only apparent life opportunity in their community—but instead will have lives of real opportunity and fulfillment.

We must build a new world by embracing the United Nations' original hope to bring all world citizens together to demand responsible behavior from our collective leaders. Leadership must create a world in which each of us and all of us are allowed to join a world middle-class society that provides ample opportunity, safety, security, and a life free of persecution and suffering.

To this end, we must demand of our U.S. leaders' actions that promote this type of cooperation and leadership. If we adopt the legislation requiring our largest businesses to move away from their insatiable profit motive to a humanity motive, we will achieve all of the following:

- Change our laws to gradually, over ten to twenty years, require businesses that import products from countries and companies, U.S. or foreign-owned, to increase, over time, wages and benefits of all of its direct and supply chain workers to a developed world middle-class level while adjusting our U.S. middle-class living standards to include everyone.

- Change workers' rights laws to protect the dignity of our citizens by eliminating loopholes in contract employment law, and creating better safety net processes that don't rely substantially on individual savings—which many don't have and currently cannot achieve.

- Change our laws to encourage businesses to invest in jobs here and abroad, creating a "produce where you sell" concept, which will broaden the worldwide market for all goods, reduce distribution costs, reduce pollution, and develop larger economies around the world.

- Change our financing and lending practices to require banks and the finance community to act responsibly on behalf of the community as a whole, affording opportunity and assistance to all, not just the wealthy.

- Hold corporate leaders accountable to long-term organizational goals, not short-term incentives. Additionally, corporate leaders must be held socially and legally responsible for business decisions that undermine the long-term health of all of their stakeholders.

- Require and assist large businesses to invest in small companies with innovative ideas that will spread prosperity to more workers and entrepreneurs to drive long-term growth and creative ideas, instead of the current approach to acquisitions of small businesses to limit future competition.

- Expand our U.S. delegation to the United Nations and Secretary of State's office to assist in leadership of the new world progress. Our delegates to these offices must encourage leaders in other countries to adopt similar concepts in their countries.

Required changes to our political leadership concept and process mind-set

More than any other change in politics is a requirement to adopt the True Leadership concept. Our Big Politics leaders must begin to understand that everything they do must be foundationally set in all of us and each of us. All legislation must lead backward toward supporting answers to questions like:

- How will this affect everyone?

- Is it going to positively affect some and negatively affect others?

- If so, who will be affected and in what way?

- If it appears to be unfair to some, why are we doing it?

- Is it a corrective action, eliminating a past benefit, unfairly giving an advantage to some smaller group than all of us and each of us?

- Is it giving a benefit to a group that is not people, but a business or organization?

Sadly, for the Republican Party, this change will be extremely challenging. Over the last few decades, Republican legislation has extended benefits to groups smaller than all of us—those at the high end of privilege or to groups that are not people, such as Big Business. That's not the Republican Party of several decades ago. Hopefully, with a significant populous movement toward the concept of all of us and each of us, they will eventually adopt this—especially if we remove corporate money from Big Politics.

I am hopeful that our Big Politics can move significantly toward the middle, where we can create a revitalized model of democracy, where our vision parallels the ideals set in the birth of our nation, and we, as Americans, will fight to forever live up to those ideals.

As I said earlier, "We the People" says it all. If we as Americans want these three words to truly mean what they say, we must choose that end. We can change that today, if we believe it is possible. We have the power to choose True Leaders who believe in this vision. Similar to the Declaration of Independence, we can change the direction of our country and our future world by demanding it, as our forefathers did. Only this time, we do it within our democratic right.

Big Politics True Leaders should begin immediately to adopt the same foundational principles that We the People will adopt to measure their fitness for office. I believe the below foundational principles must be added to our Constitution as a Citizen Leadership Bill Of Rights:

- True Leadership includes a fundamental thought on which we lay the foundation to remake our world, and that thought is "each of us and all of us."

- Who are each of us and all of us? Simple answer: We, humanity, are each of us and all of us.

> True Leaders lead from the future, embracing world sustainability without further harm, working to immediately correct current and past abuse of our world, all while building a new future economy based on people rather than only profit.

True Leaders, whether in Big Politics or Big Business:

- Lead by putting all people above personal wealth, positional gain, or business profit.

- Lead without using fear strategies and tactics to separate people from other people to garner favorable gain in the form of profits, votes, or legislation.

- Lead by serving all people with fairness and equity when it comes to life's essentials: air, water, food, shelter, safety/security, energy, information/communication, education, and health care.

- Lead from the future, embracing world sustainability without further harm, working to immediately correct current and past abuse of our world, all while building a new future economy based on people rather than only profit.

- Lead by partnering to solve the education crisis required for future world development and sustainability.

- Immediately join together with the other nations of the world to adopt this connecting humanitarian process.

> With today's technology, each political office
> candidate should be able to run a political
> office campaign without allegiance to a specific
> political party.

How we can eliminate our political parties

Political parties no longer serve We the People. They only serve to separate us and benefit poor leadership across the globe. This must change in the following ways:

1. Our goal must become all of us—humanity, not some of us. No automatic separation, like the smaller group of political parties.

2. We require that all politicians consider what's right for all of us, no longer "winning at all costs" like the smaller group of party politics.

3. All citizens must consider an individual politician's ideas, not party ideas.

4. All politicians must make law that serves and protects all of us, even those who want only to protect themselves or their group.

5. All politicians must create an economic system with opportunities and protections for all of us with continued prosperity for everyone. No one gets left behind...ever.

6. All citizens must understand we all have responsibility for the rest of us, and accordingly, we must mentor those who lack responsibility knowledge, and understanding for whatever reason. There is no free ride, but there is also no societal failure to help those who have slipped into desperation.

7. With today's technology, each political office candidate, with volunteer and/or paid help, should be able to run a political office campaign without allegiance to a party.

8. No longer will there be party alliances that block and undermine responsible and needed legislation. Speaker of the House—as well as a new position, Speaker of the Senate—as well as committee chairs, will now consist of three individuals, a chair and two vice-chairs—to limit power and split duty responsibilities. Speaker and Chair decisions occur upon a majority vote of the three office-holders. These positions will be elected once per year by the entire individual body of each House of Congress.

Conducting future elections for federal political office with no political parties will require:

1. All offices for federal representation of any state shall now be for the whole state, whether senator or congressional representative. The number of federal congressional representatives shall be calculated as defined by federal law with respect to population but without regard to particular state geography. State representatives will work for everyone in the state.

2. All senatorial officeholders will now be limited to four six-year terms with elections for each Senate office held as it is currently. All congressional representative office-holders will now be limited to five four-year terms with election for half of the delegation every other federal election cycle. Existing officeholders may run for one term extra beyond the new maximum years served.

3. No candidate for federal office may align with any group of any kind. Campaign contributions may come from individual donors only as new federal law provides.

4. Any U.S. citizen and state resident with proof of citizenship and residency can obtain from their secretary of state for federal elections an authorization to begin an exploratory campaign for federal office up to two years before the next federal election date. Candidates must specify the office—Senate or House.

5. Any authorized exploratory candidate for federal office can obtain computerized voter lists with addresses for all state citizens eligible to vote from their secretary of state for federal elections.

6. Any authorized exploratory candidate for federal office may then begin a virtual online Internet campaign or in-person campaign to acquire no less than 1,000 dated actual written signatures of which at least one signature from half of all statewide counties (or equivalent jurisdiction) is required from the state's list of the most recent presidential election voters. This signature may be electronically generated and submitted directly to the campaign and the secretary of state or a hard copy signature card kept by the campaign and electronically submitted to the secretary of state.

7. Eligible state voters may submit up to five such signature cards on behalf of five individual candidates seeking election to federal office.

8. Federal law relative to political campaign contributions will apply to both exploratory campaigns and actual office ballot campaigns.

9. All exploratory campaign candidates who achieved the necessary qualifying signatures per the secretary of state's audit are eligible to participate in a super runoff election for actual office to be held no later than 240 days prior to the next federal election. The super

runoff election will narrow the candidate field to four times the number of offices up for election, whether Senate or House offices.

10. Remaining office candidates will be narrowed to two candidates for each office position up for election no later than 120 days prior to the next federal election date.

11. Remaining candidates will be elected to their respective federal office on the actual federal election date. Candidates with the largest vote count for the number of open offices will become the federal officeholders.

The above will have many scratching their heads. Why am I recommending federal political officeholders all represent their entire state? Please allow me to make my case.

As discussed earlier in the book, we have significant trouble solving our most significant problems because federal politics has divided allegiances. And there are many significant issues that must be solved quickly. In today's world, we will be better served by focusing on an encompassing solution process rather than whose solution is better and each representative's specific issue.

Within the country and the world, no matter what the issue, numerous jurisdictions have an almost exact duplicate issue, especially if we focus on the root causes of the problem in its solution. We must make the process itself have the tools to solve any related issue anywhere in the country and the world. Whether the problem is infrastructure, poverty, law and order, global warming, job loss, racism, economic development, health care, pollution, energy, safety and security, education, and every other big problem, we need a process that solves it anywhere in what may be the same or different ways.

The encompassing solution process is founded on the fact that the issue and the solution relate back to all of us. None of us wants to be left out of the solution to any of our most significant issues. Politically, this type of work is hard and can be helped exponentially by increasing the number of congressional members working together to outline encompassing solutions far more than focusing only on their individual voting district. If the process is changed, solutions will come much quicker to their voting district because the process outlines the required solution outcome, not the specific details, making everyone much happier. It will also eliminate the gerrymandering problem.

Required critical legislation

Before getting into specific legislation, I believe we will achieve greater benefit from outlining, in concise but broad language, the *intent* of our most significant future laws. Similar to constitutional language, Congress must specify why the bill is being proposed, the reasoning or basis for its implementation terms, and finally, the expected broad humanity-based outcome to be achieved.

My hope for adopting this change to our legislative process is to give rise to more easily amend statutory details misconstrued in the implementation process and provide better guidance for the courts to more easily rule on the same if required. In other words, the humanity-based intent, as it should, drives significantly more timely adjustments to previously enacted legislation that missed the mark.

Accordingly, much more legislative time will be spent on wording the legislation's intent than on details of the legislation. After adopting True Leadership foundational principles and Futuristic Sustainability, legislation based on intent will hopefully bring us together and speed the process of required law and less polarizing debate. As part of the Futuristic Sustainability package, even funding should come to Congress as recommendations for a problem's solution.

Big Politics True Leaders should immediately begin work on proposing legislation to remove all corporate and special-interest money from Big Politics and limit individual contributions to specific candidates, while also creating an aggregating limit amount of contributions to all political candidates, political parties, or any other politically affiliated entity. In the future, only contributions from individual people may be made to any political candidate, political party, or any other politically affiliated entity. Additionally, all political contributions of any kind shall be disclosed.

Big Politics True Leaders should immediately begin work on proposing legislation to remove lobbying of any kind from any source, the legislators of the United States' Congress, and the president of the United States. Congressional True Leaders should then immediately begin work on proposing legislation to create industry groups' citizen members. As discussed earlier, the industry group citizen members will regularly meet with their Big Business, Big Politics, and Big Government counterparts. These industry citizen members work for We the People, not Big Politics and Big Government, or said another way, not Congress or the president. The purpose of the industry group meetings is to facilitate recommendations to Big Politics and Big Government regarding Futuristic Sustainability, long-term plans, discussion, and execution of required legislation.

The next significant legislative requirement will limit Big Business's profit motive as its dominant motive for decision-making by categorizing business into big and small businesses. Big Business must be required to move away from the common stock market, the reason for its short-term decision-making. Additionally, Congress must create a requirement to change Big Business's funding mechanism to preferred stock, no market, and long-term debt. Finally, Congress must create the category of nonprofit societal-needs big businesses that will operate in the marketplace with no income tax liability. And Congress must remove profit only based incentive compensation from Big Business corporate executives, moving it to achievement benchmarks of long-term plans.

Unfortunately, we have seen too much bad behavior and self-centered behavior at the highest levels of Big Business and Big Politics. Accordingly, we must create criminal legislation with mandatory sentencing of top-level Big Business and Big Politics Leaders who violate the law's intent by enriching themselves or injuring people they are leading. For crimes such as corruption, detrimental collusion, gross negligence, etc., mandatory sentencing should be fifteen years with no opportunity for parole before eight years to dissuade the act in the first place or correct it as soon as it is discovered. Additionally, all personal physical assets acquired in the enrichment or injury process shall be confiscated and/or available for restitution. We must no longer give our top-level leaders a pass card on their bad behavior. It severely undermines our democracy and our business ethics.

Finally, we must begin to create the Futuristic Sustainability model for the United States by authorizing and mandating its existence within the Constitution of the United States. I realize this is not an easy requirement, but it is essential to our future as a nation and a world. We cannot allow any future politicians to throw out the permanent connections we desperately need between Big Politics, Big Business, and We the People in our fight to solve both our significant issues and our world's vital issues. Throughout the book, I believe I have shown the ironclad need for much stronger bonds between our democracy, economy, industry, society, and education. We must cast it in the Constitution of the United States of America, giving Futuristic Sustainability just power in foiling future leaders willing to cast the connections aside for their benefit.

Recommended changes to the office of the president of the United States

We all observed the presidency of Donald Trump and his ability to eliminate the checks and balances of our democracy by using the single executive power of the presidency. Over the last century and prior, we have also seen the ability of authoritarian leaders to use the media—the printing press, the radio, the television, and now the Internet—to build their power base with distortions of the truth in their quest to conquer the world. Like past authoritarian leaders, Donald Trump was a master at using the media to create misinformation that undermines democracy.

The power of the presidency has been growing since our country was created. Because of the sheer power our forefathers gave it to provide for our safety and security. George Washington, skeptical of the singularity of presidential power, served only two terms. He feared the presidency's influence could lead to a king mentality and undermine our democracy, leading to presidents elected into perpetuity. By his action, Washington set an unwritten two-term limit precedence until Franklin Roosevelt ran for a third term at the beginning of World War II and a fourth term just before the end of the war.

Until now, in the mind of our presidents and our congressional leaders, a bright red line existed, never to be crossed: the president worked for We the People, all of us.

For many of us, by his blatant actions, Donald Trump shined a negatively bright light on the presidency. Like never before, he removed many cabinet members and career government employees from their positions, generally, for not agreeing with him. That type of leadership in any organization is not right for moving the organization forward. It significantly undermines our concept of democracy when only "yes men" remain in positions of authority. We must now evaluate whether that type of power in one person's hands is reasonable and safe for all of us and each of us. Trump has shown unequivocally, how close we could get to an authoritarian leadership executive branch of our government.

Is that what we want going forward? I think not.

My suggestion is a three-person executive team, serving a six-year term with a maximum of two terms, elected by the people in rotation every two years. I believe this system, in addition to True Leadership and Futuristic Sustainability, will virtually eliminate the chance of authoritarian rule. That's not saying that if We the People decide we want the government's executive branch to make all the rules for our life, it can still happen, with the election of three executives in a row with an authoritarian strategy for leadership.

The highest level of operation in the new executive branch, as it is currently, has to do with laws and executive decisions. Bills of substance—not operating and correction bills—must be unanimously agreed to by all three executives. In the future, Congress should approve and change operating and correction bills on its own without executive approval, assuming the operating and correction bills arose through the constitutional Futuristic Sustainability process. Similarly, executive decisions would be the same: unanimous consent. Emergency decisions, in today's world of technology, should not be a problem.

The most successful small businesses I encountered in my decades of business consulting had a team of leaders driving the growth of the company. The least successful had one leader making all the growth recommendations and approving their own recommendations. In scenario two, there was always a glass ceiling preventing future growth because one individual's breadth of knowledge is always limited. Also, their egos tend to get in the way of the best decisions.

> When Futuristic Sustainability is driving the process of change, connecting everything to everything and changing the office of the president to a team of executives, we should finally begin to see the world President Kennedy saw in our future in 1961.

With this new executive branch process, I believe we can get a much more functional and operational federal government system, connecting better with our federal government's congressional system. The oversight executive role can be split between the three executives, but all three can help each other evaluate all cabinet recommendations. Congress can mandate this shared process within the requirement of unanimous consent of substantive votes and decisions.

The goal of the federal government should be to work for We the People. When Futuristic Sustainability is driving the process of change, connecting everything to everything, and changing the executive office to a team of executives, we should finally begin to see the world President Kennedy saw in our future in 1961.

Concrete evidence supporting the change in the presidency came in the form of legal action taken to require Donald Trump, while president, to provide information he refused to deliver in two separate cases in front of the Supreme Court. As part of one of the issues, Trump's attorney attempted to make the case that, as the only branch of government represented by a single individual, the president of the United States should not be required to respond to any legal actions. The Supreme Court, for the most part, shut this argument down immediately. However, the fact that the president believed there was a defensible position allowing for an "above the law" circumstance while in office is one step away from authoritarian leadership. Maybe the next president will win that argument. We need a change in the executive branch of government.

Free market versus Big Government

In our political fights, we often have a narrative pitting Big Government against Big Business—or as it's often put, free-market against Big Government. I hear all the time that business is more efficient than the government: "Business can do it cheaper," and other similar comments.

If that is the case, in my mind, business can do it all—except control of the price by exchanging the profit motive for an effectiveness motive. Remember, there must be profit almost all of the time, or the business will cease to exist. But profit cannot be the single or overpowering motive that it currently is for Big Business. Let's move to a "what works best" motive. We can have several businesses motivated by working on the same expanding benefit problem, competing and collaborating on behalf of all of us and each of us...a continuous "what works best" concept.

The effectiveness motive hits the health care issue head-on.

A Medicare alternative or Medicare for all may work, but how and why should Big Health Insurance, Big Pharma, and Big Providers continue to make so much profit on the backs of people? Under either proposal, the system remains intact. The cost will continue to rise because there is no check on efficiency and effectiveness. The system must be changed significantly to force a new objective for health care: humanity.

What if we eliminated the profit motive by requiring all health industry businesses to operate as nonprofits, then leveled the playing field by requiring all large health insurers to write the same insurance in all fifty states, adjusted for market? Next, moved the employer-paid adjusted current benefit to its employees as wages to eliminate the disparity between the lower cost large employer self-insured plans and individual/small employer plans through the Affordable Care Act. Finally, all of us should be given a tax-deductible premium deduction for the entire premium. Subsidies for the poor would be carried over as-is from the states and federal government for now.

Big Business is not the enemy. Business, like money, is a tool. Its narrow motive is the enemy.

I can virtually guarantee that this plan will be much cheaper than either of the standing proposals within three years. And because it retains its employee base but replaces its profit motive with a humanity-based continuous best-concept motive, the industry can finally move in the right direction to control costs and improve benefits over the long term. How? By connecting with the other health care industry, big businesses can make real progress toward better health care outcomes for all of us. We only need you, our true political leaders, to be courageous enough to get it done.

See Appendix 2: Health Care for All of Us for more details.

We all need the funds to pay for basic life-sustaining needs

Let's review Maslow's Hierarchy of Needs:

- Air
- Water
- Food
- Shelter
- Safety/security
- Energy

And my added needs:

- Education
- Information and Technology Tools
- Health Care

Many of us are financially secure and can pay for the above basic needs and a few luxuries. But even in this nation of great wealth, millions of families live in poverty, barely scraping by from paycheck to paycheck. These families often have to decide which is more important: paying the electric bill or buying groceries.

When a family doesn't have the money to provide for their basic needs, the rest of us step up and help. Some of us do that through donations to charities or active participation in organizations that help the needy. Others feel that the poor are responsible for their financial situation and must find a way out of poverty on their own. But the fact is, no matter which group you belong to, and whether you want to or not, you are subsidizing those who live in poverty and are struggling to meet their basic survival needs.

Subsidies are often included in the prices we pay for goods and services. We are often unaware of a business's support, either through its commitment to a charity or legal requirements, which contributes goods and services to low-income families. Either way, the rest of us pay higher prices. In addition to charity and price support of the poor, all of us taxpayers are well aware of our subsidies to the needs of the poor. Some of us are okay with that, and others are not. You may vote for politicians who promise to cut taxes by eliminating financial help to those who live in poverty, but that won't solve the problem. We the People have decided that we aren't going to let people in this country starve because they can't afford to buy food, so one way or another, the rest of us will be helping them provide for their basic needs.

But that's not the end of the discussion. With all of the above said, we must ask a question, "Is it fair that someone puts in a day's work, whatever their job, same as the rest of us and can't pay for their needs?" I think not. As you have heard me say many times, we are all human, and the work done, by each of us and all of us, should provide for our needs. So the follow-up question becomes, "How do we change the system to create that outcome, changing government and charitable subsidies into real wages?"

First, let's make an observation from our current pandemic, Covid-19. We learned early on who were essential workers and who weren't. They were those who worked the fields and factories that produced our food and toilet paper. They were the truck drivers and store personnel who delivered, stocked, and sold our food and toilet paper. I use "toilet paper" tongue in cheek to drive home my point. Many of these workers work for less than a living wage. The job we do does not matter; all of us are essential workers for some part of our economy. We all deserve the respect that comes with a living wage. We must begin to understand the difference between a living wage and subsidies and charity. We need all of us to create and deliver the world's goods and services, not just those of us that make the most money.

Once we accept as foundational the deserving nature of a living wage, we can begin together to create the transition to that process. That transition starts with where we are at and moves forward over time to accomplish the change. Because everyone will not agree with whatever the solution, most of us must stand prepared to fight for the plan. Solving this type of problem forever must come out of the Futuristic Sustainability concept. It will not come from our current political process, which only creates short-term partial solutions reversed by political power leadership change after the next election.

Economic and tax policy

Whether paid directly or paid through taxes, the bottom line on paying for anything is that We the People pay.

You may be thinking, *That isn't always the case. Businesses also pay taxes.*

Businesses do not pay taxes. *We* pay the taxes they owe in the prices of the products or services we purchase from them. I'm not talking about sales tax, which we pay too. I'm talking about their income tax, property tax, and any other tax they pay to any government agency. We the People pay it indirectly. There are no business taxes. Any discussion about any business tax is a red herring.

On the other hand, many of us have a misconception that prices will go down if business taxes go down. That would be nice, but it rarely, if ever, happens. Instead, the tax break goes into the pockets of the shareholders of the business. If business taxes go up, we pay the taxes. No matter what, we pay.

I am not in favor of any tax incentive policy. Lower taxes meant to encourage businesses to invest in jobs and/or new products or services does not work. Most of the money goes to buy back corporate stock and add, every year, to company profits.

Smart business persons and wealthy individuals invest in new ideas that can create jobs, but not because of a tax incentive. They invest because the timing and expected return on the investment is worth the risk. Deciding to invest in new ideas and jobs solely because of the tax reduction simply does not make financial sense. Most big businesses used their 2017 tax break to buy back stock, meaning that we individual taxpayers got stuck with the cost of the tax reduction with no resulting benefit, while stockholders and executives made off with our money.

For the tax breaks to be invested in growth, Big Business must be assured the change is permanent—no reversals of tax benefits by the next Congress or president. However, the 2017 corporate tax break should never have been offered and passed without a matching business conditional investment. It needs to be a double-edged sword: no investment, no tax break. We the People still want the investment in jobs and new ideas, but we must get it, not just a promise…or worse, no commitment at all.

This is a perfect example of why Big Business, Big Politics, and We the People must be connected in this process and why tax incentives usually fail to produce a positive result in jobs and new ideas. In the future, We the People must be at the negotiating table.

We must make this type of deal work for all of us and for Big Business to build a sustainable future. Only it must be a fair deal with long-term goals and plans. It can be done. But the intent of the deal can't be bypassed by unscrupulous lawyers and Big Business executives. The lawyers and executives must be given jail time when they thwart the intent of the law. We the People are tired of this behavior.

Personal tax reductions almost always go proportionately to the wealthiest individuals, who are also supposed to invest in jobs and new products or services. Like business, the wealthy don't use their tax savings to invest in jobs, new products, or services. History tells us that tax cuts rarely increase future tax revenue because of higher business profit and higher wages—the lie we are fed to support a tax cut. Just the same, we are often duped by our Big Politics leaders using tax cuts to generate votes. Even when we middle-income taxpayers get a small increase to our paychecks, the combination of tax reductions, both corporate and individual, leads to significantly higher federal government deficits, the resulting missing tax revenue plus interest. Inevitably, our children and grandchildren pay for the tax cut, a cost-shifting mechanism used by deceptive political leaders.

Tax collection systems

There are many ways to collect tax revenue. Because of my background, I have seen almost all of them. The best understood and generally more likely to be accepted ways to raise tax money for the "businesses" governments provide are the ones matched well to the services it provides. Those taxes are called use taxes—auto registration, highway tolls, and fuel taxes for funding highway construction and maintenance; real estate taxes for funding roads, sewer and water, schools, and local government. Another generally accepted tax category is specific benefit taxes like Social Security and Medicare.

However, the largest by far category of taxes is called general fund taxes. The most common and generating the most revenue are an individual income tax, a corporate income tax, and very often, a value-added tax (similar to sales tax). These taxes support most of what the government does for us. Many of the services the United States provides are services that help us, people, even if we individually don't participate in them currently or get a direct benefit now. Services like education, the military, FBI, immigration, border patrol, air traffic control, airport security, Secret Service, Medicaid, housing assistance, food assistance, environment and pollution control, highway system, post office, national park system, and the list goes on. Our individual income tax funds significantly all of the above. Corporate income tax also contributes significantly toward them.

Many of these benefits we do not use currently because we do not always need them. Nor in many cases will we ever directly need them. An example is our space program. Although we do not directly need it, it has been a significant reason for our technology explosion.

Many other countries have a federal sales tax. It's generally called a value-added tax. Its application is slightly different from sales tax, but we can think of it as a sales tax for our purposes. In many countries with this type of tax, the revenue generated accounts for a significant share of the country's total tax revenue. In all countries, there are multiple taxes. There are many other taxes, such as wealth taxes, estate taxes (slang calls it a "death tax"). As you can see, taxes can be assessed on almost anything.

A free-world currency

As part of Futuristic Sustainability, a single free-world currency will be the best way to connect everything to everything. Let me make my case by outlining several of the significant reasons.

- The world has gotten smaller because of technology, transportation, and global issues: global warming, shared security, shared economy, and shared world catastrophes.

- Competing big businesses and Big Industries will now become collaborative.

- Funding solutions to world issues should be funded by a combination of public and private funding connecting industries and businesses best suited for solutions.

- By connecting economies of the free world countries, we will solve some previously unsolvable world problems and coordinate the solutions in encompassing better plans to target poverty, income disparity, hunger, global warming, and many others.

- Global monetary and tax policy at the highest levels will now focus on stabilizing policies that begin to solve significant disparity issues between everyone.

> If we link our Life System disconnects between people and countries, we can use the single free-world currency and monetary and tax policy to help begin to solve these disparities.

Let's begin by talking about democracy around the world.

We are seeing many former democracies sliding back into authoritarian leadership of some kind. Venezuela, Turkey, and Brazil have slipped, or are slipping, along with others.

Even the stronger democracies like the United States and several European countries are dealing with more nationalist idealism. Why is that? Simple answer: many of the people of those countries, even our stronger democracies, have been left out of the prosperity of their country. Unscrupulous leaders then exploit the fears with lies to gain more unjustified power. The reality lies on the other end—a tenuous world economy laying waste to the lowest levels of world populations because too much of it is based on materialism. It's out of balance with Maslow's Hierarchy of Needs.

Now, suppose we link our Life System disconnects between people and countries. In that case, we can use the single free-world currency and monetary and tax policy to help begin to solve these disparities over a relatively short period—twenty to forty years, about the time it will take us to solve global warming. How? We have many problems not currently being solved by our focus on the luxury/materialistic portion of our economies. The Maslow part of our economies should be getting a lot more attention, translating into significantly more jobs. For most of us, it represents 70% to 80% of our spendable income. For many of us, it's 100% or more.

We need more and better infrastructure. We need more and better food production, nonpolluting. We need more and better energy production, nonpolluting. We need more and better-connected education institutions because of the required new jobs. We need more and better nonpolluting transportation solutions. And the list goes on, and these solutions are required all over the world.

The stronger democracies should be exporting vast amounts of knowledge, expertise, and manpower all over the world. But we are not because we are stuck in a world economy that focuses on luxury and materialism instead of people.

Let's get our heads out of that "place where the sun don't shine." Connect the money to the people, not the profit, by establishing a single free-world currency and a global monetary and tax policy system and begin solving these issues now and forever.

We can even strengthen and spread democracy around the world by linking it to True Leadership and Futuristic Sustainability. True Leadership requires the understanding that all of us matter, with no separation of people of any kind. Therefore, dictatorships aren't acceptable. There is always separation in a dictatorship.

Chapter 12

Big Business Leaders Must Become True Leaders ...and Lead Now!

"Leaders aren't born, they are made. And they are made just like anything else, through hard work. And that's the price we'll have to pay to achieve that goal, or any goal."

– Vince Lombardi

Business is a tool to support people in their quest for a better life

Commerce is the process of trading something for something else. I believe that commerce is the most significant concept created in human history. It allowed humans to segregate our daily activities into categories of activities to meet our survival needs. In the early days of commerce, each of us chose daily activities that we were best at and traded the fruits of our chosen work for those fruits of others' labor. Some of us were farmers, some of us were hunters, some were builders, etc.

Business, like money, is a tool to facilitate commerce transactions, nothing more and nothing less. Businesses, whether a single individual or groups of individuals, exist to create a more efficient means to make trade in some type of product(s) or service(s).

> When a business becomes its own reason for existence—maximizing profits—it has failed its fundamental reason for existence.

One example of early business's created efficiency might be as follows. Several farmers near a village grow various kinds of crops—corn, beans, and carrots. The business buys each crop from each farmer and sells any or all three to villagers. Now, imagine the extra time a villager would have to expend to travel to all three farmers to buy what they needed from each. The value of the business to the villager is in the efficiency of his food purchasing process. Supermarkets of today provide this same service.

New businesses often create an enhancement of some product or service never before offered. In centuries past, nearly all trade was for survival needs, food and shelter. Today, commerce is in almost anything we can dream of.

Although businesses consist of people working together to make trade, businesses are not people. Businesses are a tool to be used to support people in their quest for a better life. When a business becomes its own reason for existence—maximizing profits—it has failed its fundamental reason for existence.

Today's Big Business is failing its fundamental reason for existence. It does not care about its customers, its suppliers, the community it serves, or its employees. Employees are paid as little as possible. Its customers pay as much as possible. Communities are pitted against each other for substantial tax incentives to locate in their community, often significantly more than any resulting revenue from the influx of employees, and suppliers are left out of the equation because the needs of the big business are satisfied by foreign companies. All of this adds up to more profit and another increase in stock price.

It would be great if CEO's of Big Business began to turn the ship around by becoming True Leaders and collaborating to recommend changes to the federal laws that require a new process of doing future business. Profit can no longer be the sole driver for decisions. We the People of the world, each of us and all of us, must be the significant driver of future business.

Required critical changes to the Big Business process

It's time, Big Business, to change:

- Your motivation, from short-term profit to visionary organizational growth.

- Your funding mechanism and measurement, from stock price to fixed return.

- Your leadership incentive plans, from short-term pay-outs to sustained investment/ returns.

- Your political funding and lobbying for concessions/ handouts to investing in solutions for all.

- Your reason for existence: from profit to humanity.

That last one is probably the most important. It will require:

- Expansion of business opportunities that are based on benefits for all of us, not just some of us.

- Long-term collaborative strategies that will bring in much-greater investment capital and close the cost-shifting loophole.

- Refocus on long-term opportunity (investment) for all vs. maximizing short-term return for a few—which allows for cost-shifting.

- A significant monetary commitment into education/
  training of all of us, all the way down to preschool and
  up to retraining of employees from eliminated positions.

- A binding together of required connections between
  industries to protect and enhance the lives and health
  of us and the planet.

If we look again at the list of the ten catastrophic disasters mentioned in Chapter 1, it's easy to see that Big Business is directly involved in most of them. None of the most serious—global warming, China's rise, Russia's meddling, data attacks, wealth gap, economic meltdown, non-true business leaders—are on their way to a solution. And any one of them could change our lives forever in a bad way. Just think of two of them ongoing today for context: global warming and the costs that are ringing up every year in lives and money, and the 2008 recession creating trauma and economic loss: jobs, homes, retirement, and savings.

And now we can add the Covid-19 pandemic. Big Business will again say this is not their mandate. And I will say they are the only ones that can make a difference massive enough to help We the People save the world.

Big Business must begin to read the future and then change the future for the benefit of all of us. To do that, Big Business must immediately see that all our various industries—manufacturing, agriculture, mining, retail/wholesale, energy, information technology, education, waste management, social services, financial services, health care, entertainment, transportation, construction, news media, travel, resources and environment—even as diverse as they are, are connected.

> Big Business is shifting product costs to future generations of consumers and taxpayers because the cost of resource damage is being shifted from one generation to the next.

How Big Business is shifting costs to future generations

You'll notice that the last industry I mentioned above is resources and environment, which consists of reclamation, preservation, and toxicity. You may be thinking: *I've never heard of that industry*. In fact, it's the most significant missing piece in our new sustainable world economy. We are killing ourselves and our planet with our inaction to create a substantial industry separate from, yet connected to, our planet's production industry.

Our resource providing and using businesses—Big Oil, Big Mining, Big Agriculture, Big Health, Big Waste, Big Chem, and Big Manufacturing—have enough raw material coming out of the ground at much cheaper pricing than should be the case. Our current system is what I call a Big Business cost-shifting process. The big businesses are shifting higher future product cost and/or life-threatening issues to future generations of consumers and taxpayers—our children and grandchildren. That's because no cost is assigned to resource damage, consumption, reclamation, restoration, recycling, or disposal. All of us pay for business success in the form of government spending (taxes) to clean up ignored costs. Cost is shifted from one group to another or from one generation to the next.

Cost-shifting always benefits one group to the detriment of others. Generally, the benefits go to stockholders, executives, and financiers of one group, usually similar businesses. Cost-shifting is not a competitive thing. Often groups of related businesses get together in the form of an association to lobby governments to give them favorable treatment over others: taxpayers, employees, communities, smaller companies, individuals, suppliers, and even customers. Another cost-shifting scheme is Big Business location deals with cities, sports teams, and corporate operations.

Cost-shifting is a perfect example of the cozy bedfellow situation between Big Business and Big Politics. Global warming has been created because of a failure to enact mandatory legislation to avoid its worst consequences.

We, the voting-age people, have to take responsibility for the mitigation cost passed to our children and grandchildren. We have refused to force Big Business, through our legislators, to take responsibility for all of its business costs. We must change how Big Business operates. They must operate from Futuristic Sustainability.

The need for continued innovation

Nothing I'm suggesting will change the prospects for entrepreneurs to reach for the stars. High-risk startups like Google, Facebook, and Amazon are still free to court angel investors or private equity groups to fund their early growth opportunities. Only when they have proved themselves over the long-term, with revenues and profits in the billions, would businesses be subject to the financing changes discussed in this book—which should be precisely the time frame to continue their entrepreneurial strategy the rest of us need from them.

It does limit the ability of mega-corporations, senior executives, and stockholders to get richer and richer by doing nothing meaningful for our overall economy. They currently restrict their own corporate growth by pocketing needed capital for stock repurchases instead of repurposing that capital into meaningful new ideas, new products, and new markets—real new ideas, real new products, and real new markets, not reworking the same old ideas, products, and markets. The largest corporations will now be forced to do what they refuse to do: invest in people for the long term. The world has many growth opportunities, but only if these mega-companies change their investment behavior. They have the investment collateral to break out of their boxes and change the world, but they will do that only if we change the funding mechanisms discussed below.

Big Business's new funding mechanism

Big Business must change its funding mechanism away from common stock and increasing profit to sustainable growth and investment, coupled with a reasonable, sustainable return by connecting with other big businesses in common goals and strategies. They already have the workforce and capital to begin this change. They just need to change the level of risk by changing their decision-making from short term to much longer term. Big Banking, Big Financial Services, Big Politics, and Big Government must help change the funding mechanism.

Once the funding mechanism is changed, profit will be removed as the only driving factor in corporate decisions. It will still be a significant but not an absolute element in decision-making. Profit will always be required to maintain organization stability and growth. Still, Big Business's movement toward the goals of its long-term plan will become the prominent driver of its ability to fund its future, similar to what we see in some of our most significant Big Business success stories: Microsoft, Apple, Google, Facebook, Amazon, etc.

All of these businesses have become very successful only to get comfortable in their current mode of operation. The funding mechanisms, the high-risk venture capital, and IPO's (Initial Public Offerings) contributing to their original growth will no longer work because the stock market will not allow it. The common stock market works on short time frames: months, days, minutes, and seconds.

We need our American, and the world's, can-do ideas to be re-adopted by our largest companies with the most reliable track records to recapture their lost ability to attract needed capital to fund their dreams.

The missing connecting pieces to propel Big Business back onto its original platform of innovative future ideas are:

- Very long-term strategic plans.

- Collaborative efforts between all industries, government, and We the People

- Move funding from common stock to preferred stock, which is not traded on any stock exchange, and long-term debt.

Big Business has cash and employees to start this process but will not take this step until the legal actions are instituted by Big Politics and Big Government to limit their transition risk. Big Business True Leadership must recommend that Congress and the president eliminate its political funding ability and its lobbying. It must recommend tying its own hands.

For our big businesses to successfully invest in long-term futuristic sustainable ideas, they must fund them without the typical high-risk, high-reward mechanism of the current stock market. We must take the handcuffs off them and allow them to dream again. This time, the dream of creating a world where each of us benefits from their commitment to a better life for all of us.

> The volatility associated with common stock is a huge distraction for Big Business leaders and drives them to make decisions around only those things that increase the short-term price of the stock.

However, that requires the move from short-term stock price decision-making to long-term Futuristic Sustainability planning. Like the Federal Reserve Bank and its European counterpart, our largest businesses must be able to limit their financial risk. Those two institutions focus on the stability of our economies. Big Business leadership must be able to concentrate on futuristically sustainable ideas.

Hence, my recommendation away from common stock. The volatility associated with common stock is a huge distraction for Big Business leadership. It drives them to make decisions around only those things that increase the short-term price of the stock. If we think about it from our own life experiences, when negative outcomes continuously bombard us, we become gun shy and begin to do nothing. We become comfortable in our own lives and do not want to change. That's the life of a Big Business leadership team: don't change for fear of the stock market's downward trend.

Only the largest businesses must be required to move to different, more stable funding mechanisms of preferred stock and long-term debt. The combination of the preferred stock, which does not fluctuate in price with the ebb and flow of market conditions, and long-term debt will give the company stability. It will allow the company to make required long-term investments in research, development, and initial production costs in their quest to make real their dreams for our future without the fears associated with short-term stock prices. The preferred stock will give the company a base of equity to build the company's overall Futuristic Sustainability plan. Long-term debt will provide the company needed project-based investment capital to complete their dream ideas.

The preferred stock must be offered at a fixed price per share (in my view $100 to make dividend calculations and purchases easier) and a guaranteed annual dividend, which is paid quarterly somewhere between $4 and $10 per share. No trades will be allowed in the stock except to pass the stock to relatives in the event of the owner's death, exchange shares for new shares, or purchase/sell transactions between companies as approved by existing shareholders and a government regulating body. The company may issue additional new shares with the same fixed price and dividend or a new fixed price and dividend to increase equity capitalization upon the same two requirements. As always, dividend payments follow interest payments in financial troubles, and dividend tiers of multiple preferred stock issues shall be paid oldest to newest. Debt would still be paid first in any bankruptcy.

The initial preferred stock offering will replace the company's existing common stock, rounded to the nearest share count and value of both. The share exchange date and time will be set by the company's board of directors within a regulatory required exchange date no longer than five years from the regulator's notice. There is no requirement limiting smaller companies from changing their funding mechanisms to this method.

This required stock exchange program will create volatility in its common stock price until completed. Therefore it is incumbent on the company's executive team and board of directors to do three things to limit volatility:

1. Spend a significant amount of time developing the Futuristic Sustainability plan for the company in conjunction with their industry and other connecting big businesses.

2. Set the exchange rate for the stock for stock transaction at values that make sense.

3. Blend the transaction with a long-term debt plan.

Let's talk about that long-term debt plan. In most cases, long-term debt will be required to achieve the goals of the company's Futuristic Sustainability plan. Long-term debt of ten, twenty, and thirty years will not be uncommon. Similar to preferred stock, no market will exist for the debt. The same rules will apply to debt that applies to preferred stock. Unlike the preferred stock, the debt must be paid off at the end of its term or refinanced. In most cases, the debt will carry an interest rate lower than the preferred stock dividend rate because of its bankruptcy preference. I would anticipate rates of between 2% and 8%.

Once converted, these big businesses are no different from any other business. Their operating plans, exclusive of stock price, must drive their decisions: pricing of products, employees required, timetables for plan execution, revenue generation and costs of revenue, earnings retention, etc.

Different is the combined motives for solving problems relating to humanity, along with profits. A profit is still required regularly, but not necessarily quarterly, maybe not even annually. The company's plan could forecast losses for some time while it meets the goals of its plan. However, if that is the case, the company's plan should show sufficient cash and equity to meet these and future goals. Ultimately, just as with today's common stock funding system, continuous unplanned losses will lead to the company's failure. Losing money undermines solving the problem because sooner or later if you can't fund the solution(s), you go broke. Therefore, the long-term operating plan must be well thought out and adjusted if needed, with the combined motives in mind.

Another major piece of funding is a need for additional capital, preferred stock and/or debt, for financial issues or changes required to meet new commitments for its role in Futuristic Sustainability. For this type of offering, a new updated long-term plan will be provided at least three months in advance of the actual offering date with projections for revenue, costs and future profitability, timetables for progress and completion of new and existing commitments, and all particulars of old and new offerings and retirements of preferred stock and debt.

To secure 100% of future required investment capital, these transactions will use bid market prices on the offering day only. The face value of the offered security will be used for calculations of preferred stock equity, dividend payments, debt, and interest payments as long as the offering reached its fundraising goal. Failure to garner the required future investment capital will necessitate regulators, financiers, and appropriate industry committee members (Big Politics/Big Business/People reps) to evaluate the shortfall. That group will make recommendations to management on the next course of action, including several varying and/or combination solutions. If this is the case, all offering money received will be held in trust until a resolution is determined, but in no case longer than ninety days. The money will be returned if the offering is not part of the resolution.

Adverse outcomes, including financial issues, should be less likely because of Futuristic Sustainability's connected operating process. Futuristic Sustainability aims to continue to progress to the future solution, taking into account everything needed in each endeavor. In other words, money is no longer a make-or-break issue, giving us more flexibility in solutions. We will find the money that solves the problem or moves us closer to an ultimate solution instead of past decisions in which money often canceled any possible solution.

This process works because Futuristic Sustainability forces all parties to work together to achieve the best possible outcome, not one that allows Big Business to reap excessive profits off the backs of taxpayers and citizens. The solution is tied to Big Business needing some profit and its employees needing jobs. Benefiting people/organizations need a solution. We taxpayers/citizens want it solved for a reasonable price. And maybe the world needs to avoid a catastrophe.

Let's continue this discussion from another direction.

Earlier I talked of the need for Big Finance to use its money power to promote Futuristic Sustainability. Because everything will be connected, funding of needed transactions may also be connected. Financing for a Futuristic Sustainable operating plan for multiple big businesses may now come in simultaneous funding transactions with several lenders, brokers, and even the world's governments. That's not to say that all funding transactions would be this connected, but it will now be possible for that type of outcome.

Even though there will no longer be the need for market condition brokerage, Big Finance—banking and brokerage—will still be involved at the front end of transactions earning reasonable fees for ideas and setup of needed funding transactions. Also, ongoing informational support of investors will always be required. Smaller annual fees in the realm of 10 to 25 basis points should cover the cost. Without a continuous market, the cost of fund management is substantially reduced.

Additionally, dividend and interest returns are now fixed for the term of the investment. Jumbo investors may be able to invest directly with the offering company without any management fee. Fiduciary/ trust institutions within Big Finance can invest in all transactions and split their investment with smaller investors and institutional investors to earn ongoing investment management fees of 10 to 25 basis points, similar to today. I suggest Congress set low-end reasonable management fees for Big Finance. Big Finance can split its congressional approved fees with smaller brokers if so desired. There is too much profit, as it is, in this industry. Since the risk is being reduced, the profit should be reduced.

Additionally, a huge side benefit of the change in Big Business funding is a less-volatile market of investments, especially in the retirement market. In my opinion, both interest and dividends should be deductible business expenses for corporate tax purposes. We want these big businesses to succeed, so let's give them every chance. As they are today, interest and dividends will be taxed as income to the recipient, unless in a retirement program.

The new economic and investment model for mega-corporations

What if all big businesses began working together to create out-comes for Futuristic Sustainability? As an example: What if Big Oil began working with Big Utilities, Big Transportation, Big Energy, Big Technology, Big Information, Big Chemicals, Big Education, Big Manufacturing, Big Finance, and Big Waste and maybe more, to first brainstorm about new more cost-effective and environmentally safe ways to transport us, keep us cool, keep us warm, convert waste to future use products. Secondly, this collaboration could draw up research and creation plans for all of the involved industries to be used in the long-term financing plans of planned solutions to wean the world off of oil as a fuel for transportation and energy. In the world of the future, oil will be much better as a raw material source for plastics. Big Oil could, if it wanted to, be a source of funding big businesses in the move away from fuel. This is an example of one of the hundreds of major futuristic sustainable idea processes.

> If all of the Big Health businesses were genuinely interested in the care and longevity of all people, we would see an immediate removal of the profit motive from the entire health care system.

Another example: What if Big Health Insurance began working with Big Providers (hospitals, clinics, doctors and nurses, technicians), Big Information, Big Technology, Big Pharma, Big Education, Big Government, and all of Big Business to find ways to cut the cost of health care to the levels of other developed nations while increasing the level of care and increasing the longevity of We the People. I suspect that if all of the Bigs were genuinely interested in all people's care and longevity, we would see an immediate removal of the profit motive from the entire health care system. Health care is an industry, same as other industries, in which its players point to each other as the cause of the problem. There is always enough blame to go around, but there is never enough collaboration on solutions to price/cost/profit reductions.

Because of the short-term profit motive, we don't focus on anything that does not produce a considerable profit. We desperately need answers from the drug industry for some of our most common ailments, including Alzheimer's/Dementia disease, diabetes, influenza, and antibiotics. The drug industry's fear tactic,—"Don't reduce our profit, or we won't be able to create new drugs"—even though the drug industry, historically, has some of the highest profit percentages of any industry.

We desperately need the Bigs in this industry to collaborate on solutions, not work competitively for profit. This includes much more research on holistic solutions—drugs and other things we already find in nature. Currently, there is limited money in comprehensive solutions, so there is little supportable research. We need a new kind of health care system in which the answers and funding are collaborative, not competitive.

If we change the leadership structure and the capital structure to align with True Leadership and Futuristic Sustainability, the opportunities are endless. We just need to help Big Business take away their current economic handcuffs.

The largest global companies, the financial industry, and potential market bubbles

According to the Forbes Global 2,000 list of the world's largest companies, the United States still has more companies than any other country. China is catching up but still behind. My hope for China is that they will join the free world of democracy soon, at which time they will become a full-fledged partner in solving the world's problems rather than a well-entrenched economic competitor of the free world. I hope that China's leader, XI, sees soon that leading for the freedom and benefit of all of the world's people go hand in hand. Unfortunately, he appears to be going the other direction. He should look more closely at his country's last two hundred years of history. Sooner or later, people want democracy. They want a say in their destiny. He could give it to them and be remembered in history forever.

Getting back to Forbes Global 2,000, the numbers are staggering in revenue and profits when summing all of these companies. There is so much money available in just these 2,000 companies that it's obscene, but most of it sits on the sidelines doing nothing, in my way of thinking. These companies are enormous and employ millions of people, but they all have already made their financial mark on the world economy. Most are now trying to stabilize their growth and stock price. We need them to reinvest in the future world from their strength and knowledge by linking together with their financial position counterparts.

The most profitable industries on the list are Big Banking and Big Financial Services. These industries continue to be a significant roadblock to moving from stock market/profit-driven economic development to long-term futuristic sustainable economic growth. Their pressure on stock price reporting drives no real Big Business investment in people-based long-term futuristic sustainable economic development plans. Instead, it continues to drive short-term profit-driven decisions, the likes of which created the crash of 2008, bubbles created by Big Banks and Big Financial Services asking, "How can I make money quickly with little or no risk in this market?"

> Currently there are two looming bubbles, similar to the last recession, which only need a small economic panic to set them off.

Big Banks and Big Financial Services don't typically lend to Big Business, except short-term credit, since Big Business has its own cash stash. Instead, they lend to consumers, small and medium-sized businesses, and consult with Big Business for big fees on things like stock buybacks from bond offerings and major stock offerings. They also create layered risk managing tools to mitigate their own investment risk by selling and buying part of the competitors' financial risk products—things like mortgages and other commercial lending and financial risk products. Another example is insurance of all kinds.

These same tools created the crash of 2008 because no one was minding the store, overseeing the risk product creation process and controls. All of the Big Banks and Big Financial Services Industries assumed that it must be good if their competitors were doing it. It was a herd mentality of the most massive scale ever, and we paid the price for the short-term, get-rich-quick attitude of our largest financial institutions.

There are currently two looming bubbles, similar to the last recession, which only need a small economic panic to set them off. Right now and for the previous ten years, interest rates have been so low that there is, once again, a looming real estate bubble—not quite the same as last time, but one that could be just as detrimental. In most cases, it still takes two incomes to make a mortgage payment. Any job loss by one breadwinner and a house is foreclosed on. There is also a stock market bubble poised to create a crash, just like the last one by any significant economic downturn.

I believe this bubble will burst relatively soon. Because interest rates have been so low for so long, investors have ballooned common stock value. The result is that there is too much investment in common stock relative to its relationship to other investments. Generally, other investments are interest-producing bonds, both government and private companies. If the stock market crashes, just like in 2008, there is no place to move invested money, which creates a downward spiral in stock value. As before, the Bigs will cut payroll, jobs, trying to maintain profitability on less sales. Workers without jobs begin to lose their homes. Covid-19 already created a short-term market crash. It could create a much longer one without some serious government input.

This mentality leaves other Big Business industries continuously worrying about the looming and eventual economic collapse. Hence, Big Business's no-real-new-investment and its stock-buyback mentality.

All of the above is the inevitable unfortunate outcome of an economic system that operates on a short-term mentality. We must change our economic model for our largest companies to provide long-term—decades, maybe millennia—economic stability by investing in humanity rather than profit.

At the beginning, everything mattered, especially people

All of you Big Business leadership grew up in the current economic system, the stock market in which more and more corporate profit drives every decision—because more profit creates higher stock prices and higher corporate value.

If you were one of the lucky founders of one of our

mega-corporations—Microsoft, Apple, Facebook, Google, Amazon, Tesla—at the beginning, everything mattered, not just profit. People mattered. You talked to many daily:

- Customers: "How's the product working for you? Glad to hear it."

- Suppliers: "I really needed those parts. Thanks for getting them so quickly."

- Employees: "We're doing great. Thanks for all your hard work."

- The city: "I appreciate all of the help on our new manufacturing building. It's up and running weeks before our plan. Thanks again."

Now, even if you still talk to some of those same people once in a while, your time is now focused on the current quarter's profit:

- "Are we making our planned profit?"

- "If we're going to miss planned profit, why?"

- "How come this product is behind schedule?"

- "Can we do anything now to correct it?"

- "We can't have another down quarter. What can we do to speed production?"

- "How can we cut cost?"

Once the company hits the big time, everything revolves around planned slow growth and continued profit increases. But We the People need you, Big Business leaders, to act like you did when you first began. We need your vision of the future—not just your company's future, but the world's future—and your push to connect everything to everything to make the world better than any one company can make it. To do that, we need to change your current mind-set that revolves around quarterly profits to a new way of thinking and doing Big Business Futuristic Sustainability.

Chapter 13

A Call to Action

"Never doubt that a small group of thoughtful, concerned citizens can change the world. Indeed it is the only thing that ever has."

– Margaret Mead

Our survival is at stake

Because our world has become globalized in every way, disasters lurk around every corner.

1. Global warming continuing its march toward planetary destruction.

2. Terrorists inciting anarchy and bloodshed at home and around the world.

3. China's rise in the global economy and an authoritarian world power.

4. Russia's reemergence into Cold War politics and tactics.

5. The continuing nuclear threat posed by small, non-democratic nation-states.

6. Data attacks with world-crippling power on the economy and democracy.

7. Economic class disparity holding financial influence over leaders and laws.

8. Greed of bad corporate actors capable of collapsing the free-world economy.

9. Corporate focus on wealth, creating loss and undermining institutional trust.

10. Attacks on the virtue of diversity, once again creating significant human division.

11. Finally, pandemics – Covid-19

Leadership's lack of a solution strategy for these mega problems ensures their repeated near future occurrence on a scale so massive as to undermine our very human existence. None have been adequately addressed globally or domestically.

> We no longer need leaders with ego-driven agendas, but leaders who understand that finding solutions that serve all of us and our world are the only answers that make sense.

We are in a war for our existence. We must now choose to attack these looming disasters head-on or push them aside and hope a miracle saves us from our lack of attention. It's our choice.

Our current leadership is out of touch with the future world and, accordingly, disastrously slow at predicting crises, let alone preparing for or responding to them. We no longer need people with ego-driven agendas, but people who understand that finding solutions that serve all of us and our world are the only answers that make sense.

Many ordinary young people across the globe with hope and dynamism for change in many different jobs and positions are just waiting for their opportunity to lead to be realized. If you are one of these future True Leaders, let me speak directly to you. You are creating massive informational and technological change. More to

the point, you are the futuristic young, dynamic global True Leader
the world needs now. You are being educated or working in business,
medicine, government, industry, energy, food production, resources,
finance, education, tradesman, and many more places. The world
needs your expertise, your energy, and most of all, your commitment
to each other and the rest of us.

You young leaders will use skills learned and information gathered
in this fast-paced world and demand changes to our laws and world
direction to avoid the reemergence of any of the above disasters
and many smaller ones. If current lawmakers are slow to respond,
you, the young True Leaders, and your followers will mobilize to
democratically remove those in power and replace them with your
representatives using the new tools of today's information and technology world you created.

You, our new young True Leaders, will not only be involved in
politics, but you will be the new leaders of global business, industry,
and government. We desperately need new business and industry
True Leaders who understand that there is much more than profits
that drives decision-making in the world of the future.

The need for citizen engagement

We, all of us, must begin to realize and significantly embrace that
which binds us together in our shared humanity. We Americans have
a very high degree of pride in the country we have created. But as
we have seen in brilliant and terrible color in our recent history, we
have a long way to go in linking ourselves to the ideals we created so
many years ago but not yet lived. We can no longer afford to live in
segregated and separated communities of color, ethnic background,
religion, gender, financial aristocracy, or anything else. And I don't
mean the physical places we live, but we must begin to live those
ideals everywhere in all of our life. We must become the authentic
role model for the world that looks to us for guidance by embracing
our humanity and sharing it with them.

As a practical matter, it would help immensely if we physically integrated, whenever and wherever there is an opportunity with everyone who looks different than us, who speaks differently than us, who believes differently than us, and with anyone who does anything different than we do.

We, all of us and each of us, must do our part to guarantee our continued existence. We must begin to see our humanity as a binding foundation for going forward. We must see all of our neighbors as we see ourselves.

We all have the same desire for our future:

- A prosperous economy that provides us meaningful work and a reasonable paycheck.

- An education system that teaches our children well and prepares them for the future.

- A secure and safe place to live—including a healthy planet.

- A reasonable cost to live without passing some of that cost to our children.

- And finally and importantly, freedom from tyranny from any source.

It's time we stop including our differences as the roadblock to our life's direction. Instead, we should celebrate our differences, for they are the blessing we've been given that expedites the process of achieving our goals. All that remains is for us, red states, blue states, Republicans, or Democrats, to vote for true visionary leaders who will take We the People soundly into our Sustainable Future.

The world's democratic and economic role model

After World War II, to protect ourselves from future conflicts, we, the United States, instituted the Marshall Plan. The plan both helped rebuild World War II enemy and allied economies and assisted in creating democratic political systems. The Marshall Plan process further highlighted the success of democracy as a better form of government and one that is less likely to lead to political upheaval and chaos. Many countries have since followed the democratic process lead. We are now the role model for democracy in the world. Our elections, politicians, and government are watched by all world citizens and all world governments.

In addition to democracy, many world governments have adopted our economic model over the last seventy-five years. While adoption of our economic model has benefited many of our largest corporations over the previous twenty years due to moving production to cheaper labor markets, it has, in hindsight, hurt many American workers. The adoption of the model by foreign countries is not the only factor in job loss. The growth of technology, too, has had a significant impact on manufacturing. More machines mean fewer workers.

Why do we care about the rest of the world?

> Too many business leaders are pushing their companies to the bottom of the wage scale, making it more difficult for workers to achieve a middle-class life.

First of all, as the free world leader, we must show the rest of the free world the way to freedom and democracy. Even if we believe we have no such obligation, history has shown us that our security depends on it, lest we risk the chaos and wars of the first half of the last century. Secondly, we can also learn from history the consequences of failing economies, which exclude or are unable to provide meaningful employment to large population sectors. We opened the door to more prosperity for emerging democratic countries with our trade deals of the 1990s. As a result, many of them moved away from dictators to full democracies. Shutting those doors now will create adverse outcomes for them and us. Terrorism is, in many cases, desperation, the result of nothing to do.

Another history lesson from the last century comes from Henry Ford, the founder of Ford Motor Company. He proclaimed that his employees "must be able to purchase the company's automobiles." As such, he set some of the highest wage scales of his time. This statement should ring loud and clear to business leaders all over the world. Unfortunately, too many business leaders are pushing their companies to the bottom of the wage scale, making it more difficult for workers to achieve a middle-class life. Low-paid consumers, who now represent a significant percentage of consumers, will eventually be unable to afford many items we currently produce here or in other countries. Ultimately, this will force many businesses to contract or close, leaving many without work and an untenable downward spiral in the U.S. and world economy.

We must create a visionary global futuristic sustainable economy focusing on societal needs using our new high-tech business models and systems. All of us across the globe need better answers to energy, health care, food and water, resource planning and conservation, and yes, even information technology. That does not mean we abandon our current economic model but enhance and expand it.

History again shows an example of this in the space program of the 1960s. Our present economy is built upon ideas and issues that came from our commitment to space exploration: enhancements in communications, computing, and medicine, just to name a few. Imagine what we could do if we gave that same commitment to all of our societal needs.

Investment always creates the Future

In my management career, I have spent a lifetime trying to change the discussion we all seem to have about cost to a focus on opportunity. Leaders that focus on cost only, money spent, are fear creators attempting to maintain their wealth and power. In reality, cost done properly is an investment in opportunity, almost always generating a return greater than the investment. With no investment, there can be no opportunity.

> Investing significantly in our education process is the only way we will be able to meet the needs of our futuristically sustainable world.

We cannot afford to let our focus on cost deter us from making prudent investments that will change our lives for the better. Investments come in many forms: infrastructure, buildings, highways, airports, railways, power plants and electrical grids, water purification and supply lines, waste, and recycling, etc. Most of these systems are old and need replacement. We are beginning to replace them but are often behind the curve.

Also, in my opinion, it seems we are updating them with new technology but without regards to our future world. We cannot stop repairing or replacing what is truly broken, but we must begin to look at where we are going with an eye toward solutions that prevent future breakdowns, eliminate pollution, and waste precious resources. We must start to think about all future costs and investments with an eye to the future, whether it's infrastructure, new consumer products, food and water sources coordinated with production and distribution, and everything else we need to survive and grow. We have a finite planet. We cannot wait any longer to change course.

More than any other investment, we need an investment in our children. We taxpayers—but more importantly, Big Business—must now begin making significant investments in education. Investing significantly in our education process is the only way we will meet the needs of our futuristically sustainable world.

Our teachers must be paid well and have excellent benefits. Teachers must have respect for their knowledge and the service they provide for us: teaching our children. In some schools, the burden on teachers goes way beyond just teaching. We must level the teaching burden by creating solutions that work to combat poverty, the underlying cause of this increased teaching burden. Those solutions exist, as teachers in many places will tell you. We just need to step up and push hard for their implementation.

Big Business must step up to participate in the dilemma of our current inadequate school system. Their participation can come in many forms, but every form will require a financial commitment. It should also do enormous amounts of good for their future workforce if they are involved in a connected conversation about their future needs. Big Business can no longer sit on the sidelines but must participate significantly in the whole solution to our education system improvement. Their involvement must include solutions that appear not to be education-related but are part of the education problem, such as poverty and other society-related issues.

Democracy is all of us and each of us, People First

We just went through one of *the* most divisive, if not the most divisive, election in our country's history. In raw numbers, more of us voted in 2020 than at any time in history. Yet, we must ask the question, "*Why* did we vote in such staggering numbers?" Almost all of us have an answer to that question. But interestingly, the list of answers is quite long. Over the last eighteen to twenty months, the media and political parties have been hounding many of us about that answer. For most of us, the list comes down to a combination of two interconnected answers to the following question: "Which presidential candidate do you trust to solve *your* most important particular issue?"

This answer is fundamentally terrifying when it comes to saving our democracy, our world's democracies, our lives, and our planet. Why is it "terrifying?" Because in addition to our middle split voting for our presidential leader, it says, "We the People are center split on all issues, no matter the issue." Our democracy has become "My way is right, and your way is wrong." Meaning winning, no matter the cost, is the only thing that matters, even if the cost is our democracy itself! We no longer care about what the other half of the country thinks and why they think that way. We must begin changing our behavior in order to bring HOPE back into our politics: *Help Our Politics Evolve*.

Let me begin by reintroducing our process of democracy. It's the national democracy that I believe our founding fathers envisioned, even if they didn't agree on everything. In our democracy, we make law setting rules for all of us and each of us to follow. We come about those laws by citizen voting, electing representative state politicians for the state in which we reside and a president representing every citizen of the whole country. These elected national officeholders of the two Houses of Congress, Senators, and Representatives of the House, then make the laws we live by in the United States. Each of these officeholders votes to approve or disapprove bills (if passed, law) brought to the floor of their respective Chamber...the Senate and the House. By a majority vote of attending members of both Houses of Congress, a bill passes into law upon the president of the United States' signature. No presidential signature, no law.

The process seems relatively straightforward until we ask the following question, "What *guides* the voting member of Congress and the president to vote for or against a particular bill?" The simple answer is...many things...leading to the next question, "What are those many things?" I list the most significant items below. Very interesting and discouraging is all the listed items have little to do with us, We the People. But, first, two questions to ponder when reading the list, "What if there was only one question?" and finally, "What would that question be?"

Now the list of things:

- Political party—which party is in control of the presidency and each House?
- State represented.
- Area of the state represented.
- Is the state red or blue?
- The topic of the bill.
- Whether the bill is trading political favors.
- Is there lobbying influence?
- Is money of any kind from anywhere or to anywhere involved (almost always yes—taxes, spending, campaign contributions, etc.).
- The complexity of the bill.
- The urgency of the bill.
- ...and many more.

My answer to the "one and only" question is, "Does the bill/law put People First?" above every other decision guide? And I mean, all people, not some smaller group of people. Many in Congress will say that's already the way things are. I believe most of us voters would say...We are a long way from People First solutions, given the significant unresolved issues of today.

Another question to be asked given our divided nation (and People) current circumstance, "Do we want any group less than all of us dictating everything about our lives?" A dictator dictates everything about everyone's life. Communism dictates all other citizen lives through the one smaller group, party members. Fascism dictates all other citizen lives through their preferential ethnic race group and corresponding party membership. By definition, even Socialism dictates the lives of all citizens through a community group managing all production, distribution, and exchange (community set pricing). In other words, Socialism decides everything about who gets what and for what price. True Socialism has elections. Communism, as we know it, and Fascism have no free and fair elections for all of their citizens, only party member elections. Both Communist and Fascist governments are almost always run as a dictatorship.

Democracy, on the other hand, doesn't manage production, distribution, or exchange because it isn't an economic system. However, it does set rules for how a business operates within its borders. And sometimes, because business chooses not to produce needed goods or services, a democratic government will contract out for them or do them. Rarely, at times, it will set pricing. And as we all know, it collects taxes from us in many forms for use in providing goods and services and management of our governing process. And we citizens, all of us, can elect representatives that set our governing rules.

In a democracy, we rarely have 100% agreement in the form of voting or popular support for any legislation. On the other hand, party line votes are non-productive and demoralizing for us, the voting public. Legislation should result in significantly more agreement...more like 60% to 70% agreement on almost all legislation.

Now, let's imagine a different process. Congress and the presidency throw out party politics and work for the people in an honest environment of solving problems focusing on People First. We could bring required legislation and collaborative and cooperative players together to find cost-effective long-term solutions to any problem. With a few law changes and connection between us people, Congress, the presidency, and Big Business, we can make this a reality.

Catastrophic problems...those listed early in the book...countrywide or global, must be solved simultaneously. If not, any solution is temporary at best, costly over time, and, now, life-threatening to ourselves and the planet. As an example, racism is connected to poverty is connected to education is connected to incarceration is connected to power is connected to opportunity is connected to the economy is connected to safety and security is connected to industry is connected to global warming is connected to pollution is connected to energy is connected to pandemics...and the connection feared most...is employment or lack of employment (jobs)...our wellbeing...and the connections don't stop there.

I could have chosen any example...our economy, global warming, Covid-19, terrorism, China's growing economic and world position, data attacks and misinformation in today's high-tech world, or any other significant issue. The solution is the same. We must update our most significant institutions by connecting them and us to the solution process.

I had a business owner tell me multiple times, "Don't overthink this, Steve." His business is now failing. It needed significantly more investment in operations staff training, monitoring, and follow-up corrections. Very often, we must overthink our issues to come to real and lasting solutions. I am not special. He is not special. No one person has all of the answers. Nor does a group of people focused on only their solution. Shortcut and single-focused solutions and investing too little solves nothing. We must work together to achieve the best results.

Expanding on shortcut answers and investing too little. Silo solutions and skimping on answers will not solve massive problems. World War II would have been a lost cause if we tried to fight it with no investment in arms. Similar to World War II, Covid-19, the Depression, the Great Recession...our substantial current problems will require massive amounts of money. But we must understand that *any* money spent is wasted if we do not solve the problem or move significantly toward an ultimate solution. Just as important is knowing money spent on solving significant issues expands jobs and wealth in the entire economy. Because the most extensive issues are related and must be solved concurrently, we must rework the entire concept of solutions, including funding.

Only by understanding *why* the problem exists can we begin to fix it. Most often, there are several causes of a problem, especially enormous and critical problems. But we can still fix them with much less cost and frustration if we connect the solution to the connections creating the problem. However, time is running out for some of our enormous and critical issues.

We the People are the absolute and critical factor in saving ourselves and our planet from the predictable negative future in front of us. Democracy requires each of us and most of us to share in the belief that we can and must take necessary steps to prevent our annihilation. Our problems are daunting and globally connected but not out of our control. Yet, our democracy is the solitary tool we must employ to redeem ourselves. Democracy is messy, but well over half of us (60% to 70%) must stand fast in our belief in each other over the time needed to save ourselves and the planet. We need to elect True Leaders that will help us rework the concept of solutions. There is no other course of action.

There is a plan and process that will work well if we adopt it. It requires True Leadership, and it's called Futuristic Sustainability. It was comprehensively outlined in the last several chapters.

Constitutional amendment limiting campaign contributions and lobbying

I wish I was convinced that our Big Politics and Big Business leadership would adopt the foundational ideas and process changes outlined in this book. I am not. Some of the most basic concepts discussed in the book have been discussed for years but have seen no positive movement. Just the opposite is happening. The door is opening wider to non-people influence.

Democracy is supposed to serve all of us. We the People is its sole purpose. Nothing else matters. Meaning there are no less than "all of us" groups. Accordingly, money for preferential legislative treatment of any group less than all of us must go. On the other hand, money spent to bring an equal opportunity or treatment of all of us is required. Currently, there is no business interest that represents all of us without a corresponding connection to its financial interest.

Unfortunately, we can no longer assume our political leaders will eliminate corporate and special interest funding of their campaigns and lobbying anyone other than us. Accordingly, my recommendation is, for all of us across the nation, to move forward on state-by-state legislation ratifying a federal constitutional amendment doing just that. I know this is backward from the normal process, but we need to send a message to Congress...that we want our democracy back. We must also send a message to state legislators that this is the single most crucial legislation they will vote on in their upcoming session. Again, we want our democracy back.

If we are to be successful in immediately changing the direction of our politics, we must vote for True Leaders. These True Leaders must vow to remove all money from political office elections, except limited individual contributions to candidates for the office. These True Leaders must also eliminate all lobbying except citizen groups that support positive outcomes for all of us and each of us, not some of us or some other group or organization. We must vote out politicians that continue to ignore us in favor of corporate and special interests.

We must change our election process

Political debates have been used for decades to limit the number of candidates running for the presidency of our United States of America. Unfortunately, too often those debates have turned into attacks on the opposing candidates' character rather than an informative outline of a candidate's solution proposal and implementation strategy. The political parties organize these debates and allow the media to moderate them, whose limited focus is on television ratings. In the future, if debates continue, they must be run by a nonpartisan group. Something from the past that should have remained is the nonpartisan League of Women Voters' involvement in the process, or something similar.

Debates for both the presidency and other high offices must be executed much better, but are not enough. We must begin using today's technology, creating a standardized question-and-answer format that can be videotaped and distributed to the Internet. We all must be able to see, on our own time, each candidate's answers to issues as well as their foundational philosophy on leadership, their priorities, and the direction they intend to take the country. This process will be cheaper for candidates and will allow the media to vet candidate responses for truth...not denigration of ideas, concepts, and implementation strategies.

Each candidate should also provide an Internet-uploaded open-formatted, time-limited message for higher office, where the candidate can be real with us people. We also must keep the town hall question-and-answer process to view the candidate in a one on one with us voters. The playing field of available informational formats must be the same for all candidates. All candidate messages must be freely accessible and viewable by everyone on the Internet. Meaning everyone in the country must have access to Internet technology as part of their equality of opportunity.

As we all know, the presidency is only part of the political process. The election of congressional state representatives and senators is equally essential and gets even less media coverage. This, too, must change, using similar videotaped formats described for the presidency and distributed on to the Internet for candidates seeking election to those offices.

What can be eliminated are the attack ads that run incessantly, spewing lies and half-truths about the candidate's opponent, created by campaigns and political action committees. If it were totally up to me, I would allow only political ads that promote the candidate's ideas, concepts, or strategies, meaning no reference to opposing candidate(s) in any way. We no longer need the division created by fear-scapegoating politicians in our political process.

Freedom of speech

Recently, both sides of the political divide have questioned freedom of speech and freedom of the press. Arguments about the definition of each are becoming more prevalent, and generally, based on our political party and our opinions about acceptable policy and interpretation of the law.

Hate speech is not free speech. It is meant to create fear in some of us to garner support for taking away some other group's rights. It only serves to separate us from each other for the benefit of some of us. Neither the largest nor the smallest groups using attacking hate speech are free to espouse hate toward another group.

For the most part, this entire book is my opinion about acceptable policy and interpretation of the law. With that said, I believe that the intent of policy decisions and the law should be based on our founding documents' character, particularly the words "We the People." Accordingly, if those words are our true focus, the intent is evident in all policies and laws. That does not mean creating and enforcing the law is easy, but it always gives us a measurement path back to the truth about which we must adhere: Who is We the People? Is the definition only *some* of us, or is it *all* of us? In today's world, I cannot see a definition less than all of us.

Freedom of the press and advertising

The freedom to articulate one's opinion should never be denied. Yet the truth, the facts, must never be left to speculation. Our only insurance against unscrupulous leaders and their views is an unwavering freedom of the press that points out opinions and lies versus fact.

However, the lure of advertising revenue has created difficulty in determining who the reliable press is. Advertising is always opinion, not fact. Its sole purpose is to drive us to do something: buy a product, vote for a candidate, change our beliefs. Although an ad may have some basis in fact, we cannot determine what truth is and what is not.

Through our taxes, We the People must fully fund one trust-worthy source for objective reporting—public television, public radio, and public Internet—where their charter is only us, We the People. However, we are beginning to see the erosion of public media's federal funding due to political party hostile rhetoric. Our taxpayer funding of public media must secure the truth by becom-ing a constitutional amendment. There should be no speculation as to public media's purpose. Non-tax financing from other sources is acceptable unless the funding source places conditions on the supported topic reporting.

During political campaign time, quantity-matched candidate advertising is justifiably reasonable to limit our exposure to campaign opinion ads. Money should no longer be the driver of campaign ads. We should adopt the new campaign election process discussed above and limit campaign advertising.

Why we need futuristic young, dynamic global True Leaders

The world will soon be theirs, not ours, and the world and their survival depend on the immediate action of those whose existence lies in the balance.

And sadly, I have personally encountered way too many people my age and older, too apathetic to change anything.

- "I have worked hard and just want to enjoy the rest of my life."

- "I have just enough money for retirement and can't afford any more expenses, least of all, more taxes to solve world problems."

- "I just can't worry about anything except me."

- "Everything is negative. I just can't hear any more."

What it comes down to is this: "I just don't have the energy needed to take on the daunting task of solving our significant issues of today and the future."

Again, we—all of us—desperately need you young futuristic dynamic global True Leaders. Change is coming at us faster by far than any other historical time frame. The advent of computing power has accelerated to the point where informational and technological change every ten years equals or exceeds the cumulative change in our entire human existence. For the most part, our approach to future planning is still coming from the past. This must change significantly and soon. Our computing power modeling must begin assisting us in predicting the societal future, creating plans, and implementing strategies that will avert disasters.

Our children, as we of earlier generations, have no shortage of will. Young Americans, no matter the color, ethnicity, or religion, are more than willing to step up to the challenge before them. We only need to help them achieve their dreams. Our current education system, along with prolonged poverty for too many, is demotivating. Our challenge as citizens of America, and especially us older Americans through the change to Big Politics and Big Business, is to immediately and drastically reform our education system.

Included in our education upgrade must be significantly more education time on our full history, good, bad, and ugly! Additionally, we must teach our children about their responsibility for the rest of us, their civic responsibility, and why voting matters.

In this time of great stress, we must ask ourselves, "Can we do anything more to help ourselves and our fellow citizens overcome the unending onslaught of significant issues?" As you can imagine, I have spent countless hours talking to many people over the last several years about our national and world circumstances. Much of what I have learned is in this book.

I have been asked many times while writing this book, "How do you plan to motivate people to take action to solve the onslaught of catastrophic issues?"

My answers are:

- I hope I can get them to read the book or watch the videos they can find at www.TrueLeadership.org.

- I hope they remember how to measure leadership for top-level positions. True Leaders care about all of us and know that we must connect everything to everything.

- And finally, I hope they will vote for True Leaders who understand that they must do the hard work of connecting everything.

From my observation, the polls representing our choice in presidential politics accurately portray the split in our view of solutions to significant country and world issues.

- 35% - 40% see solutions through the lens of "How will this impact me?"

- 35% - 40% see solutions through the lens of "How will this impact all of us?"

- 20% - 30% see solutions through the lens of "Who do I believe will fix the problem?"

But I've learned there is another question those of us in the 20% - 30% group ask ourselves first: "What is the problem?"

That question is the confounding question that makes it difficult to solve any significant issue. We the People in the middle must help each other get to an understanding that there is only one problem question, and that question is, "Who will fix all future significant problems before they arise." And the real answer should be, "*We* will fix *all* future significant problems before they arise." Because we want the problem solved, no matter what it is. We cannot rely on the "How will this impact me?" group to be with me or against me. So, we must vote for True Leaders that care about all of us and each of us.

Back to our children and their education. In order to immediately and drastically reform our education system, we must vote with the group of, "How will this impact all of us?" We must change to a system that not only teaches our children the necessary skills but also significantly encourages and motivates each child to become who they want to be. Remember, our children, our grandchildren, and our great-grandchildren are our HOPE for the future. *Help Our Politics Evolve*

Several new books on motivation point out that money, although an absolute necessity, is not the only motivator—nor is it, in most cases, even a strong motivator once a baseline of income is reached. Instead, we find from Daniel Pink's book *Drive* that autonomy, ample opportunity for mastery, and a sense of a larger purpose are much better motivators.

> If the rest of us are going to help our young people of the world save it, we must get out of our apathy and get involved in our politics.

We, moderate and centrist people, must get more deeply involved in politics

If the rest of us are going to help our young people of the world save it, we must get out of our apathy and get involved in our politics. Not politics as usual, but a much more robust politics. Politics, where we are engaged with each other. We must begin to understand the fears of our neighbors. In an earlier chapter, we discussed some of those fears. You will recall, almost all are due to the separation strategies prevalent in our current political climate. We must make a drive to the middle of our political spectrum.

> Town Meetings will give us an opportunity to
> listen to each other's concerns and desires.

To this end, I believe we must start a national, state, and local centrist political movement. We must bring moderate people together from both sides of the electorate. How? With Town Meetings, giving us an opportunity to listen to each other's concerns and desires.

The Town Meeting process must include urbanites and rural residents, rich, middle class and poor, Black, white, Hispanic, and Asians, old and young, business persons and workers, all religions— all categories of Americans.

These meetings will be for listening and understanding—not for party affiliation. In other words, we want people to bring their life issues and hopes with them, not their party political rhetoric. I hope that all of us will attend, even if we are party-affiliated, but then listen to the fears of our neighbors. For it is in these fears, expressed in stories that they tell, that we must begin to see our neighbors as human and equals and supporters of our democracy. We must see our neighbors as real people, not soundbites from political candidates or news media.

It is time for centrist voters who have been searching for politicians that represent them to take decisive action to listen and understand their counterparts on the opposite side of the oh-so-narrow aisle. Out of this hopeful process, I believe that we can finally bring our politics back to its roots, work together to achieve common goals, and let go of the partisan need to control the tactical strategy to achieve our common goals.

Our politicians must relearn the art of compromise or face the wrath of our centrist political power.

If we have learned anything from the 2016 election and Donald Trump's term, we have learned we are quite different from our neighbors. However, that must not dissuade us from discovering who they are and why their concerns and desires are essential. We must help our neighbors, and they must help us elect politicians who take both of us into account when passing legislation. We are all Americans, and we are one country with one overriding connection: freedom. We cannot let the tyranny of partisan politics take away our freedom.

It's time for We the People to have our own rallies

I, Steve Lundquist, will moderate the conduct of the local Town Meetings with the help of volunteers. These meetings will be virtual. The exact format at this time is unknown. However, the format and schedule will be outlined later on our website: www.TrueLeadership.org.

Our Town Meetings' goal will be for each of us, and most of us, to decide if we are ready to rally others to change the evolution of our political process. Our vital decision must be based on a sincere and honest evaluation of our own belief in our fellow neighbors'/ citizens' concerns and desires.

If we believe, we will move to Step 2 of the process: creating a new centrist political party and/or a political action committee. If we eliminate PACs, we will have won a substantial battle in the fight for our democracy. If not, we must build a PAC of monumental size in which We the People fund campaigns of centrist politicians. Suppose we collectively cannot stand by our neighbors and strive to move forward with a sense of combined political purpose for centrally solving our shared concerns and desires. In that case, we should continue Step 1, Town Meetings, until we collectively believe in our shared goal of helping our political process evolve to save our world. We are only human, with no other group affiliation.

Maybe if we listen for understanding to others with similar fears but opposite choices in party or candidate, we will find common ground for each of us and all of us to choose a single path to our future.

Summary

Foundational Concepts that Will Forever Change Our World for the Better

"Great leaders are almost always great simplifiers who can cut through argument, debate, and doubt to offer a solution everybody can understand."

– Colin Powell

The world has grown smaller and smaller, and we humans have learned much from history, especially over the last few centuries. We have learned that tyranny can't keep us down. We have always risen to take back what has always been ours: our freedom. There have been many tyrannical leaders and oppressive regimes in our history. Even in our world today, several such governments and leaders are attempting to use fear, separation, and physical terror to maintain control of their citizens.

As before, it will not work. We humans will fight, and even die, for our freedom, as we have done countless times before. Freedom to be who we want to be, not who they want us to be. They cannot take away our will to be free, nor can they physically beat it out of us or detain us at the border, or even kill us. Our spirit will live on. Nor will we let *some* of us take away or limit our life-sustaining needs or hoard them for their benefit.

Democracy is freedom from tyranny, whether it is the bondage of tyrannical leaders that use fear and physical terror to keep its citizens in line or the greed of the tyrannical few that use fear and separation by promoting and enforcing an economy that serves only them—or both. We must use our power given to us by our democracy, the power of the people, to take back and maintain our freedom forever. We must always remember that a controlled so-called "free market" that benefits only some of us or a few of us is not freedom, nor is it democracy.

And we, the free people of the world, and our democracies must assist in the fight for freedom of those who are controlled by the bondage of tyrannical leaders.

I have given examples of many of my ideas in this book to achieve the immediate change required to save our world. Many of those ideas save us from our poor choice of leaders. My ideas are fodder for thought. I hope as you have read the book that you had ideas or tweaks to mine.

All of us know that there are countless ideas for positive change to the world. But right now, I believe—and I hope you agree— that there are very few concepts that can save the world we know. Therefore, any of the countless ideas must be based on the following foundational concepts:

- We are all human. Any other group does not matter.

- We are all equal in our necessities and opportunities.

- We are all connected to each other and our planet, not separated in any way.

- We all must be free from tyranny of the few, in any form.

- We all deserve courageous True Leaders who believe, understand, and promote connecting everything everywhere will create a futuristically sustainable world for all of us and each of us.

- And right now, We the People must fight for those True Leaders.

A message from me to possible converting True Big Politics and True Big Business Leaders

I know you are out there and in positions to change the world to the world I'm describing. I also understand that this change is daunting in all respects. However, I have no doubt that *you* know I am very close to describing the required changes humanity needs now.

I ask you—I *plead* with you—to gather your courage and step up now and bring your peers with you to change our world forever for the better.

How to Solve the Problem of Global Warming

"Effective leadership is not about making speeches or being liked; leadership is defined by results, not attributes."

— Peter F. Drucker

The history and the deadline

Science has been consistently saying that we must reduce our greenhouse gas emissions to zero by 2050. Currently, energy consumption, burning of fossil fuels, coal, gasoline, related products, and natural gas represent 72% of our greenhouse gas emissions. 80% of the 72%, or 58% of total emissions, is for heating and electricity, transportation, manufacturing, and construction.

We have several other parts to attack in addition to an energy-consumption plan, the additional 42%: a food production plan, repopulate renewable resources (mostly trees and wetlands) plan, protect the planet's remaining resource plan, and a plan for other greenhouse gasses. All have the same 2050 deadline for zero emissions.

If the entire required infrastructure change system and global behavior change are not fully operational by 2035, we will not make the 2050 deadline. Significantly missing the 2050 deadline will ensure that everyone on the planet, as well as the plants and animals, will be dead or dying in 100 years.

> We must tell the fossil fuel industry to shut up and sit down...or be part of the solution by getting out of most of their industry and get into industries that will save the planet.

On top of that, we must consider the issue of methane. There is a significant probability that we will release large amounts of methane from permafrost into our atmosphere in the lifetime of anyone forty years old and younger if we miss the 2050 zero growth deadline. Methane is a greenhouse gas at least thirty times more destructive than carbon dioxide, meaning the effect will increase the planet's temperature much more rapidly than even the current projections. It's a gas; once it's out of its container, the permafrost, it's out. At that point, the best guess is, we will be beyond the tipping point toward planetary destruction. I hope no one wants to bet against that possibility by ignoring serious planetary actions now. If you do, the Big Business fossil fuel industry will take your money now and take your life and the life of the planet later.

Now is the time for We the People to demand action. We must tell the fossil fuel industry to shut up and sit down...or be part of the solution by getting out of most of their industry and get into industries that will save the planet. Coal is another major problem. Burning it for any purpose is committing suicide too.

Our current system of Big Politics and Big Business will not get this done. Several countries have only recently outlined targets on emissions, but far too few, and only after thirty years of sitting on the sidelines. The five largest emitter countries—China, U.S., India, Russia, and Japan—have not committed to anything substantive, let alone a real action plan.

We must connect all countries in a set of comprehensive plans that guarantee our coordinated achievement, including the actual emissions elimination process and the funding of that process.

The global comprehensive strategic plan

Under my plan, 2021 is the beginning of Phase 1 of the global Comprehensive Strategic Plan and continues until the end of 2035. Phase 1 is the two-year entire planning stage and the thirteen-year complete construction, destruction, and conversion execution plan.

Phase 2 begins on January 1, 2036, and continues until December 31, 2049. Phase 2 aims to fix the problems with Phase 1 because we started late and won't know for sure if we will reach the required reductions. It will most likely take until 2035 to have fully operational changes to our entire energy consumption infrastructure before we can get an accurate picture of our progress. Additionally, we must address any other currently unknown issues that may arise during the fifteen years of Phase 1. We will have just fourteen years to get the bugs out of Phase 1 until our required zero greenhouse gas emissions in 2050.

Continuing in the business-as-usual mode will undermine any chance of achieving a worldwide comprehensive action plan. Big Business's lobbying and campaign (PAC) money and the Big Politics of all major emitters, opposing economic and social strategies, will only continue to destroy any progress toward a comprehensive solution.

The global action plan for the above 2050 goal, the connection between We the People, Big Politics (especially the five largest emitters and the European Union acting on behalf of all member states), and Big Business, must be completed by December 31, 2022. Additionally, we must demand that the comprehensive strategic plan of the five largest emitting countries and the EU create their plan and commitment together because, without their combined commitment, the plan is worthless. If there is no combined commitment, We the People want to know immediately that these six world governments are the cause of humanity's and the world's demise. It's all or nothing.

These comprehensive strategic plan documents will be gathered and executed by the UN Climate Change body's representatives.

Contracts for implementation of proposed energy consumption structural changes (manufacture, construction, destruction, and conversion) by the five largest emitting countries and the EU must be awarded and signed by December 31, 2023, with work to begin no later than July 1, 2024, and completed no later than December 31, 2034. All contractors' progress will be tracked, reported, and verified by an independent body representing the people of each of the five largest emitters and the EU once per quarter, beginning on January 1, 2024.

Ten independent representatives will be elected by the people of each of the five largest emitters and the EU from a list of forty presented by the UN country (including the EU) delegation with the biographical background of no more than 100 words on each candidate. Appropriate experts and leaders are required, not political hacks. These ten representatives must operate under the True Leadership foundational principles. This process should act like the U.S./Russia space program, not the normal superpower political and economic lies and bullshit stories.

The ten should elect four of the ten to split responsibilities into three groups. The four should choose one as an overall leader. A vote of seven or more of the ten elected representatives demanding a leadership reorganization can resolve conflicts within top leadership. The remaining three representatives can choose two of the remaining six elected representatives as assistant leaders. The three leaders should hire ten subordinates for assistance with both onsite and satellite progress verification and catch-up strategy plans when lagging in the schedule. Significant administration staffing will be required.

Teams from each of the six delegations should coordinate each inspection process and work together to assist each other with any serious issues. Shoddy work, progress shortfalls, contractor conflicts, etc. are all part of the all-delegations inspection process. Reporting of progress, issues, resolutions, and necessary changes will be made to the UN delegation every quarter for review, discussion, and approval. Each country's representative delegation has broad authority in exercising its oversight duties, from coordination of the process between science, industry, government/people, and individual businesses to awarding contracts and, as discussed above, work inspection.

Salaries should be $170,000, $150,000, $135,000, $100,000, all in U.S. dollars, and relate to the overall leader, group leader, other representative leaders, and subordinate team members. (I chose to outline salary amounts to give no reason for conflict and remind these True Leaders of their single focus on humanity and the world. The salary amounts are not as crucial as their consistency of application between countries.)

The top team of four will report to both the UN and their own government. Government interference in the process or side compensation must be reported by any of the six delegations immediately to the UN. This specific progress and enforcement process will be the test of each government's resolve to support the future of its people and the people of the world. We the People do not want any cheating on our future, not anymore. That's a thing of the past.

As part of their original plan, each government will have already funded the inspection process and committed to funding its execution with guaranteed additional funding to achieve the targets. No long-term funding commitment means no commitment. All other contracts for the remaining greenhouse gas reductions specified in the comprehensive strategic plan must be awarded and signed by December 31, 2025, to begin no later than January 1, 2030, and completed by December 31, 2035. The world's remaining countries will implement a similar process with smaller staff—probably three top leaders, with a similar relative size organization, with the same timetable and lower salaries—equivalent to lesser emission responsibility.

The futuristic strategy solution process for energy consumption

All of us must understand the world is not the same as it was. We, humanity, need a new Big Politics and Big Business process to solve global warming and other significant issues. Adopting Futuristic Sustainability, with everything it encompasses, will significantly grow our world economy in all sectors, especially those in societal needs industries. On the other hand, singularly solving global warming will create a worldwide economic collapsing bubble. Huge Big Business profits and required buildups of workers and their resulting layoffs will ensure the bubble's collapse, our current way of doing business.

Beginning with that understanding, let me outline my strategy. We have five parts to energy consumption:

- Heating
- Electricity
- Transportation
- Manufacturing
- Construction

All consume fossil fuels, including coal. We must attack all of these simultaneously if we are to meet our timetable goals. Accordingly, the business process must come from Futuristic Sustainability and True Leadership. The global warming solution, manufacture, construction, destruction, and conversion must be completed by 2035, showing measurable evidence of significant future greenhouse gas reductions. We need time to react to unexpected issues to meet the final 2050 deadline.

Remember the five pieces, institutions that connect our world: democracy, economy, society, industry, and education. And remember the long-term solution concept, 30 to 100 years, not short-term

Band-Aid fixes that don't work and often create more problems. We must connect everything about this process to everything else lest we end up with global warming unsolved or solved but replaced by another big problem, or worse, several other big issues.

There's a lot of work to be done, but we can do it all simultaneously. There is no magic to it once we adopt the concepts of True Leadership and Futuristic Sustainability. They are very straightforward unless we think there is any reason whatsoever not to base our future world on humanity and the planet.

Legislation discussed in the book must be passed, even some of the constitutional amendments. Once a substantial number of world governments adopt the new legislation, we can begin talks on world currency, monetary and tax policy, which will go a long way to a funding strategy to defeat global warming and other significant issues.

The first parameter of sustainable solutions to global warming and our world's other significant problems is: do not ignore their threat to us, or opportunities for us, for any reason—not money, not time, not probability, not "it's someone else's problem," not for "I don't care about it or them" and currently, but hopefully not much longer, not spin from Big Politics or Big Business, not for any reason!

Connected organizations

Below are the institutions and industries that must come together to generate solutions required to meet global warming goals and deadlines. The elected team of ten specialists (or three in the case of smaller countries) and their subordinates from each country will lead the coordination process between science, industry, government/people, and ultimately individual businesses and contractors.

We must make sure the plan will solve the problem. Ideas from all parties must be presented, discussed with other connecting businesses, evaluated for effectiveness—reductions of GHG (Greenhouse Gas), priced, approved for implementation, and contract generation.

We the People representatives, government representatives, and legislative representatives AND Connected creation industries.

All industries listed are worldwide industries...because it's a world problem:

- Gas and electric—heat and power industries
- Commercial, industrial, and residential property owners
- Auto manufacturing, including new mass transit vehicles
- Trucks and buses manufacturing
- Airplane manufacturing
- Airline industry
- Shipping industry
- Travel industry—cruise lines
- Train manufacturing
- Parts manufacturing—all types
- General contractors—all types
- Subcontractors—all types
- Construction equipment manufacturing
- Construction materials manufacturing
- Ship building manufacturing
- Engine manufacturing—all replacement types
- Steel manufacturing
- Aluminum manufacturing
- Other metal manufacturing
- Plastics manufacturing

- Electronics and technology manufacturing—all types
- Battery research and manufacturing
- Waste, scrap, and environment pollution solution technology
- Solar manufacturing
- Wind manufacturing
- Hydro plant manufacturing
- All construction including plant and infrastructure construction
- Appropriate engineering and architecture
- World Bank (world currency) and/or government banks (Federal Reserve Bank)
- Private investment banks
- Fossil fuel industry—new connections to the world without your main product
- Accounting, audit, and laws to protect Futuristic Sustainability
- Connected transition funding—consumer and business replacement purchases—subsidies and/or tax credits, world governments and/or world bank and private investment banks

Funding the attack on global warming

The current system of funding an encompassing solution of this type won't work. The reason: the players are disconnected from the solutions they are trying to achieve. Governments are disconnected from other governments because of leadership arrogance and the long-outdated misconception about "control of their destiny."

Industries are disconnected from other industries, even from other businesses in their industries because, similar to governments, they believe they control their destiny. The economies of each of the countries are vastly different, with vast differences in their ability to undertake these global requirements, including their ability to fund the undertaking. Finally, as represented by their government, the people of each country have so far not made global warming the priority humanity's and the planet's existence deserves.

Nature, in the form of global warming or Covid-19, does not care about Big Political or Big Business *control*. It does what it wants...when it wants. We...all of us and each of us must begin to understand this. However, as I have said and will say again, we have the knowledge...we just can't wait until disaster strikes to begin to solve the problem. The day is coming when reactive solutions will not work for that moment's crisis. If we wait much longer, global warming may be that unsolvable crisis.

We can fix global warming, and all other global issue funding, by tying the funding together under one roof with a set of laws and policies. Similar to the EU, we will create a global currency and monetary and tax policy system. Along with the money system, we will create an international legal system that finally addresses Big Business operating systems and processes around the world.

The leaders of the six largest polluters of the world can solve this quickly by prioritizing working together to attack global warming.

Possible utility solutions for global conversion

Thirty percent of the entire greenhouse gas reduction must come from the utility sector by 2035, including the required increase for transportation conversion infrastructure and new consumption.

Utilities, people, governments, manufacturers, and contractors should decide what can and can't be completed in our time frame. On the table, player discussion of utility infrastructure, both existing and new, based on future demand and eliminating current polluting

plants. Also on the table, discussion about existing and future building types, new required building codes and converting existing
buildings away from fossil fuel heating. Our visionary thinking
must include underground structures requiring less heat and cooling;
mini-power utilities for pockets of similar use buildings; individual
structure power and heat; and thousands of other possibilities.

> To solve global warming in the time remaining
> before 2050, we need millions of new employees
> across the planet.

We must think fast, but we also must think smart. Many of the
old ways of doing power and heat are now in the trash can. We must
now create our new way of doing power and heat for the foreseeable
future. Because we have learned much about our planet's fragility,
we must remain diligent about how we interact with it. Who knows?
As we attack global warming, we may discover currently unknown
ways of powering and heating. The presently unknown may become
the futuristically sustainable way of living. There are no barriers to
"people and planet first." For now, we have two years to create a
utility plan that powers and heats our future world.

Transportation—global conversion

Another *thirty percent of the entire greenhouse gas reduction must
come from the transportation sector* by 2035. Below are possible
transportation solutions:

- Cross-country travel must change as fast as possible
  to high-speed (200+ miles per hour) electric passenger
  train travel, eliminating short-haul air travel, except
  for trips over 2,000 miles and overseas air travel. Or
  experimental non-polluting short-haul aircraft must be
  converted into reality in less than seven years.

- Electric freight trains must become higher speed (100+ miles per hour) and operate in restricted corridor spaces. I do not believe this technology exists, but it needs creating for high-speed timely goods distribution. For freight, I know there are both weight and climb issues. Both need addressing.

- Separate rail line corridors for passengers and freight need constructing. A system of X's and north-south and east-west corridors should get passengers and freight close to their destination with a quick spur transfer to a high-speed train to the center city. Rail transportation must become the cheapest way to move cross country for both people and freight.

- City travel must incorporate concentric circles and spoke electric medium-speed train systems that bring people to the center city and between suburbs, either above ground or below ground, similar to subways and elevated trains. Driverless electric small buses and cars will deliver people directly to home, business, or shopping and dining.

- Car travel will move to only electric cars and small trucks. With the advent of Covid-19 and technology, more work will be done at home. However, travel to one's place of business will now be achieved by public transportation discussed above.

- Land from many of today's freeways will be modified for train travel, combination travel, or extended-trip driverless car travel to nearby cities, towns, and rural areas.

- Trucks must become electric too. Most are on their way to becoming driverless and will use the existing and remaining freeway system, occupying only one lane at prescribed speeds in their delivery activity and making room for other vehicle types. Delivery vehicles, where applicable, may still have a passenger rider to assist with the delivery process. Trucks will also connect to rail freight and operate in the same corridor space as high-speed freight trains.

- The need for electricity will accelerate once these transportation changes are beginning implementation. Significant electricity projects must be undertaken simultaneously to meet this increased demand: solar, wind, hydro, focused sunlight, and batteries. Fusion power is now something that should be vetted thoroughly and implemented or dropped. New fission should be vetted too.

Solving global warming in the time remaining before 2050 needs millions of new employees across the planet. We need new trades men and women building or modifying the required infrastructure: dams, railroads, power plants, residential heat, and power conversion systems for buildings of all types, new types of traffic corridors—around cities, through or around mountains, all across the country and the world, and many other green construction projects. We need millions of factory-working line employees to build or modify the required transportation systems and energy storage systems. We need new green food production methods and technology that produces more on less land with less water, doesn't pollute, and—under significantly variable planetary circumstances, maybe even production in winter climates—and distribution systems that match that goal. New food production methods will require many more farmers and production workers.

Everything above will require more researchers, engineers, scientists, and, finally, True Leaders for every aspect of global warming solutions. And this is just the start of the opportunity for millions of new world employees.

With the immediate and significant need for new employees on many fronts, we will require significantly more, different, and better education processes. Just as with the other institutions of Futuristic Sustainability, education must rise to the challenges of tomorrow very quickly—not in its silo, but in a new and better-encompassing process. It must partner with Big Industry, Big Government, and We the People to create a lifetime of education that fits the business and industry needs while allowing people to flourish throughout life.

This whole scenario is outlining the significant issues we must address to solve global warming. The details buried in the solution will seem endless, but all of those details must lead us back to the required result of zero greenhouse gas emissions by 2050. The task may seem daunting, but if We the People remain focused on holding our world leaders accountable all along the way, it is solvable.

As we see in the global warming example, True Leadership will help us solve most issues. But True Leadership and Futuristic Sustainability are really about building the life system process that solves problems and issues well in advance of their catastrophic impact on us, not the current system of reactive problem resolution. Almost all of our issues are known. It's a matter of courageously leading by leveling with us about the solutions. Then we, each of us, must lead, follow, or get out of the way of the required resolution. We can no longer be the reason for poor top-level leadership.

Health Care for All of Us

*"If we have no peace, it is because we have forgotten that
we belong to each other."*

— Mother Teresa

I bought health insurance for many small companies over my
forty-year business career. Both my wife and my father were senior
executives in large health insurance companies. I know the *Whys* of the
problem from both sides. The following is my summary of the issues.

There are two significant problems with our health care:

1. It's unaffordable and/or inaccessible to many people.

2. Health care businesses like making a lot of money,
   especially insurers.

These two requirements are at odds. The left wants to throw our
tax money at the problem. Under the left's scenario, prices continue to rise whether we pay in higher taxes or the higher prices of
health care providers. There is absolutely no incentive for affordable
care. The right wants individuals to pay; accordingly, if you can't
afford it, you don't get it. Same arguments on almost every political/
business issue.

Let's define it in health insurance jargon:

- Guaranteed Issue—Insurer's can't refuse to cover anyone. If you're sick, this is critical to you.

- Mandate—Everyone must buy insurance, or a government program must subsidize those who can't afford it. This benefits business.

These two issues were the general compromise between business and the people in passing Obamacare, the Affordable Care Act, to balance the cost equation. The insurers said they needed more money to cover sick people, so they asked Congress to require all people to pay some health premium (individual mandate). The individual mandate is similar to states requiring that everyone driving a car must have car insurance. If you drive a car without insurance, you pay a fine or go to jail. If you don't have health insurance, you get an income tax penalty. The Affordable Care Act passed entirely along party lines: Democrats for it, Republicans against it.

The right repealed the individual mandate as part of the 2017 tax bill because they had pushback from many younger voters and others who, in general, are in good health. The young didn't want to pay for health insurance, especially if they were in a low-paying job. Others didn't want to pay additional taxes for those who could not afford the new coverage—the compromise legislation between Democrats and Big Health—mandate and subsidy in exchange for guaranteed issue.

The guaranteed issue is still in place as I write this, but the political right is trying to get it thrown out in federal court. If successful, that would completely repeal the Affordable Care Act to, in their mind, balance the equation. In effect, this would bring us right back to where we were before the Affordable Care Act, thus no permanent solution to health care.

Health care for all of us—the issue in summary

Let's talk in more detail about health care. From our side of the issue, it's all about cost. It's too expensive. Why?

1) There are many required players in the industry.

   a. Insurers

   b. Doctors and nurses—specialists of every variety and some generalists

   c. Hospitals—some general and some specialty

   d. Drugs and medical devices—research, manufacturers, and distributors

   e. Clinics—numerous for every possible issue

   f. Research facilities of all kinds—cancer, diabetes, Alzheimer's, etc.

   g. Suppliers—drugs, medical equipment, medical supplies

   h. Emergency medical services—ambulances, etc.

   i. And more

2. *We* don't need them most of the time.

3. Yet *all* of the above stand ready all of the time.

4. And *all* of the above will only do what they do if they can make money, both

   a. Businesses

   b. Employees

5. Finally, *we* only want to pay for what *we* need.

Although all of the above is not news to any of us, it is necessary to focus on the list in order to grasp the magnitude of the cost problem. So the real question is, "How do we pay for something we don't need most of the time, yet have it available when needed all of the time?" Especially when what we need, when we need it, is often a life-and-death issue.

The short answer is and always has been, all of us must pay something all of the time for something that is required almost never. That answer is called insurance. However, to get the full picture, we must ask three other questions too.

1. How much should each of us pay?

2. And, what if some of us can't pay that amount?

3. And the last question, can the cost, how much we pay, be reduced?

Now, let's look at Obamacare, ACA—Affordable Care Act. Why is something that should have answered the above three questions not working for everyone? Typically, Republicans see ACA in one way, and the Democrats see it in another way. Accordingly, as stated previously, the answer is significantly harder to explain than you might think, but let me try to answer as simply as possible.

The short answer is ACA insurance premium more than doubled a similar prior insurance premium. Additionally, the young believed, "I'm healthy. Why do I need to pay for something I don't need?" And low-wage workers could not afford to pay any premium, let alone a very high premium.

Now more details. The more than doubled insurance premium. Rural America and its low-wage workers are, for the most part, Republican and angry about Obamacare's negative impact. So, too, are small business owners anywhere for the same reasons. Before Obamacare, premiums for health care in rural America and small business were reasonable. Now they have more than doubled. Why? Coverage increased but only slightly better than before. The real increase came as a result of the preexisting condition exclusion being eliminated. Insurers raised rates significantly to cover the unknown health of their *new* insured population, their perceived unknown risk. Prior, if you had health issues, you just didn't get coverage. You were rejected. Now insurers can't deny you coverage. So insurance premiums skyrocketed. Insurers now make good money on ACA products. But ACA price has effectively cut out much of the intended market for insurance, especially the young and healthy and low- and middle-wage earners and many small businesses. That's why many are mad. They don't qualify for subsidies; they pay much more or are not buying insurance because their financial circumstance does not allow it.

Why the significant impact on rural America? Rural America is farmers and small businesses or big businesses that generally do not offer health insurance to low-wage workers. What was once affordable because the sick were excluded is no longer affordable. For the most part, workers in rural America paid for their own health insurance. It did not matter whether you were a farmer, a small business, an employee of a small business, or an employee of a big business that did not offer health coverage.

The only rural Americans that did not feel the negative impact of the price increase in health care were government workers, state, city, county, and education workers, and some well-organized employees of larger businesses. Why not these people? All of these organizations are self-insured because of their size. ERISA health care law and the marketplace allows them to run their own insurance program, which they fully fund for direct out-of-pocket costs, and they know the health of their employees, reducing the unknown issues.

Additionally, if one of these large organizations has an employee with significant health problems, that employee is generally indirectly forced out of their job because of missing work. Often they have disability benefits encouraging their departure. Accordingly, large employers' pool of insureds are more static, predictable, keeping their health insurance costs closer to its predictable historical values.

The above issue is the real issue in health care. Big Business and Big Government, because of how our system is set up, get a substantial health care benefit. Big Business and Big Government still pay between 50% and 60% of the equivalent ACA policy price. The rest of us can only dream of that price! Again, why? The Bigs fund their own insurance because they know indirectly who is sick and who is not. Regular insurance will not take that risk, leaving farmers, small businesses, and individuals to pay much higher premiums than the Bigs.

There is now one other problem that arose after the repeal, in effect, of the mandated premium requirement of the ACA. The mandated premium requirement said everyone must buy insurance or suffer an income tax penalty. With the penalty removed (changed by Congress to zero), people who can afford the premium will only buy in once they know they're sick. This change will continue to raise ACA premiums higher and higher until the only people using ACA will be newly sick, previously uninsured individuals, and taxpayer-subsidized insureds. ACA is no longer sustainable without significantly more federal funding. Sooner or later, ACA will collapse from the weight of its recent unsustainable program changes.

How much should each of us pay?

And what if some of us can't pay that amount?

And, the last question, can the cost, how much we pay, be reduced?

The above three questions are still there. Why should some of us pay more than others for the same coverage? Maybe for age or financial circumstance...certainly not an employer. What if we can't afford it no matter what the cost? Can we cut the cost? In general, we should not pay more just because we don't work for the right organization. Nor should we go without health care because we are a low-wage worker, farmer, or small business owner. Finally, we can lower the cost but not with Obamacare or a single-payer solution. With either program, the gate is still open for significant price increase manipulation by all the players in the process.

My solution is outlined below in detail and is based on the above facts.

The basis for agreement

- Federal law, not state law, will insure comprehensive, fair, and equal health care for all of us.

- Health insurance pricing will be based exclusively on the age and the home geography of each of us.

- Each of us and all of us will be responsible for the cost of our own health insurance (some will be subsidized).

- Government assistance—federal and state, if appropriate, would be issued as credits to our insurance premiums.

- Nationwide competition and collaboration of federally licensed health care businesses will drive down costs.

- Reserves, not profit of health care businesses, will insure long-term, not short-term, solutions to health issues.

- Health insurance net of government assistance will not be taxable under federal tax law.

Leading to these foundational principles

1) The new national health insurance program must be federally mandated and regulated, and all licensed insurers must write insurance coverage in all of the United States.

2) As individuals, not businesses or government, we must be responsible for our own health care by choosing our insurance plan, insurer, and pay for it (some will be subsidized). Current employer health benefits would be rolled to employees as wages, and the entire premium would be tax-deductible.

3) Health care businesses (insurers, providers,

manufacturers, distributors, etc.) must be nonprofits to limit short-term solutions to long-term health issues.

4) Pricing of health insurance must be based on specifically mandated health insurance products adjusted for only age and geography without regard to employment status or government subsidies. No opt out. Everyone in...All of us pay and/or are subsidized.

5) Bad actors in pursuit of fraudulent (or unjustifiable costs/prices of) health care business or contributing to excessive health care costs should significantly contribute to the solution and/or spend time in prison.

Health care for all of us—recommendations

1) The health insurance industry, along with all other health care businesses, will now be licensed and regulated by the federal government under authority from Congress. As such, all health insurance and health care businesses will not only be allowed to operate in all states, but health insurance companies, in particular, will be *required* to operate in all of the United States and its territories. It is expected that there will be at least eight to ten of these new national health insurance companies arising from the conversion process of existing health insurers and appropriate new and consolidated companies.

2) All of us must acquire health insurance from a new national health insurance program. Cost of the insurance will be a direct reduction to your federal taxable income. Under the conversion to this program, if your employer currently provides subsidized health insurance to you, they will be required to maintain paying

that current benefit to you in the form of salary or wages. Self-insured employers would pay 135% of the calculated benefit to cover insurer profit previously only paid by small employers. Employers could pay you more than the current benefit but not less than the current benefit. Calculated benefits would be prorated to match age-related premium payments. Employers would be audited for this calculation as part of ERISA benefit audits. As stated above, you will be allowed to deduct the full amount you pay for the insurance from your federal taxes. This should not be a significant hit to tax collections, since most of us are employed, and we are not taxed on our health insurance benefit. Those of us who don't currently have company-provided insurance will now be able to deduct its cost on our tax returns.

3) Each individual (or family unit) is now responsible for their own health insurance premium. Families must buy insurance coverage from only one insurer. Employers can implement an administrative premium payment process if so desired. Such a process must be available to all employees and make payments to all insurance companies. A maximum discount to such employers of 2% of the premium paid will be allowed to an employer for their aggregating administrative payment process.

4) Medicare and Medicaid recipient premiums will be paid to the insurance company by either or both the federal government or state government less any premium due by law from the Medicare or Medicaid recipient. Similarly, state assistance programs will be paid directly to the insurer.

5) Move all health care businesses (insurance companies,

hospitals, drug, medical device/equipment and service companies—manufactures and distributors, etc.) to nonprofit status with provisions for conversion of existing businesses and creation of new businesses.

6) Regulate the drug and medical device/equipment industry to provide United States insurance companies and providers like hospitals and doctors with the lowest world price for their products. (Will be audited by government or government contractors.) This will be the highest value paid by any insurance company, hospital or doctors' clinic, or individual in the United States for medication, device, or equipment. To provide for long-term cost containment and elimination of market manipulation, insurance companies will no longer be allowed to own other health care businesses.

7) Conversion of existing health care businesses into nonprofits will not be without some issues. However, most can be converted with some minor law changes. The current common stock of for-profit companies can be converted into new (and/or consolidated) companies with dividend-paying preferred stock and debt (no market). Current stockholders of such companies could choose a cash buyout or conversion of common stock to a preferred dividend-paying stock or notes and bonds, or a combination of both. Issuance of new preferred stock or bonds to cover conversion or future investment capital will be a part of this process. Regulations will be created to limit the profits of investment bankers involved in this conversion process.

8) Limit CEO and other executive team member compensation packages of health care businesses by regulation to fixed values and long-term (10 years

plus) progressive incentive pay, not short-term incentive pay.

9) Congress will create seven categories of health care: Preventive, reactive and corrective (routine), chronic, catastrophic, accident, mental and addiction. Each of the seven categories of health care will be defined by regulation authorized by Congress. All of the seven categories of health care will be incorporated into the new national health insurance program.

10) Pricing of health insurance products will be determined by Congress and appropriate regulation using the seven categories of health care. All insurance companies will be pricing specified products consistent with this regulation so as to make comparison shopping by consumers uncomplicated. All of us are required to purchase all seven categories of health insurance unless you are deemed low income or a small business by regulation. If so, you will still be required to purchase all seven categories of coverage. However, subsidies, direct payments, or tax credits would be made available from federal or state programs to fund missing category coverage. Subsidies will be paid for by all of us as part of our total monthly premium. This category separation will allow Congress (not Big Business or insurers as in pooling) to tier premiums (in the form of government subsidies) of low-income individuals and small businesses. This way, everyone still pays the same premium. Only some of us have backside credits/subsidies approved by government action. This is an essential feature because it lets us know the gross cost of our health insurance regardless of any subsidies. The few individuals paying the gross insurance cost on their own should not be the only

people who know that value. We are all accountable
to each other and must know this number.

11) Pricing of health insurance will be determined by
each individual insurance company based on their
ability to negotiate costs of provider contracts with
hospitals, doctors, preventive care businesses, chronic
care businesses, addiction facilities, etc. as well as drug,
device, and equipment providers as well as innovation reward incentives to those same providers and
five years of paid claims history plus debt retirement
and preferred stock dividends, interest and justified
investment reserves adjusted for additional insureds.

12) Each insurance company will also determine pricing
based on the age of each individual buying coverage
with no regard to preexisting conditions. Families
would be the sum of the age pricing. The regulation
will define age-pricing brackets and limits on pricing
for older participants.

13) Pools of business (or categories of business) will no
longer be allowed in the calculation of premium pricing…only age. Insurance companies will include all
of us in one pool of users along with the total costs,
reserves, etc. of the whole company in the calculations
of premium pricing by age bracket. Bracket pricing
must be progressive and fall within corridor guidelines
discussed below. Additionally, pricing will be calculated without regard to any type of group-affiliated
status. Any discounts offered to any group or organization (other than the employer administrative payment
process discount) will indicate grounds for all persons
insured by said insurer to receive similar pricing.

14) Individual pricing must fall within an overall price

corridor of low and high price set by regulation by geography so as not to allow market manipulation...buying or dumping business. To this end, as discussed earlier, licensed insurance companies must price, promote, and write coverage everywhere and anywhere in the United States and its territories. Pricing can reflect specific market characteristics of costs but must be priced using overall business profitability (i.e., no pooling by market or age).

15) To promote competition and protect the overall health insurance market, no health insurance company shall be allowed to have more than 30% of the market of insureds in any geographical market and no more than 20% of the overall U.S. market of insureds. Regulation shall be created to adjust currently (every year) using corridor pricing by market to realign each market to achieve the "no more than 30%" of market insureds and if required, to adjust currently (every year) using corridor pricing to limit any insurance company from controlling more than 20% of the entire U.S. health insurance market.

16) Insurance company reserves for future and unpaid claims will be calculated as in current industry practices but in no way to exceed three years of paid claims history (adjusted for current insureds) plus debt retirement, preferred dividends, interest, and justified investment reserves. Excess values over the above must be used to reduce product pricing.

17) Deductibles, copays, and lifetime maximums will no longer be allowed.

18) The ERISA large employer exclusion of state compliance issues will be eliminated by virtue of the new

federal law because each individual is now responsible for their own insurance premium. This eliminates the burden of state-subsidized insurance coverage for some individuals paid for by taxes on only individual and small business insurance premiums. States and the federal government can now add cost to geographic insurance cost to all of us in the geography (with no exclusion for large employers) to recover some cost of subsidized insurance coverage.

19) Under the new health insurance program and health care business legislation, any business that is found by a federal court by jury decision (new or old) to create products detrimental to the health of our population will be assessed annually a tax to fund health care costs associated with such health deterioration until such time as the product is removed from the market or declared no longer detrimental due to a product modification. The amount of tax shall be calculated by the CDC taking into consideration all public health costs as well as the negative effects and costs of potentially moving such products into the black market. These funds must be used by Congress to fund health research and/or defray public health spending.

20) Under the new health insurance program and health care business legislation, individuals or organizations (represented by senior executives) found by a federal court by jury decision to defraud (or unjustifiably inflate costs/prices for significant profit) individuals, the United States government or its taxpayers in the pursuit of any scheme involving a health care or health insurance business shall serve no less than three years and no more than twenty years in federal prison.

Why these recommendations?

1) Federal government regulation—health care should be a right that all of us can enjoy in an equal and fair process.

> Large insurers preferred over smaller insurers operating in all of the country. As discussed later in an example, large insurers, due to their size, will have buying power (cost reduction) across the country, lowering their financial risk below that of localized small insurers. Additionally, the federal government's administrative and enforcement cost of market regulations surrounding product pricing and market manipulation will be substantially less with fewer insurers. That does not preclude small insurers from becoming linked to large insurers to achieve the same result...the conversion process. Administratively, the large insurer will be responsible for the smaller linked insurer's regulatory requirements as they apply to the large insurer's small insurers market and countrywide requirements.

2-4) Move health care acquisition responsibility to us (not employers or the government.

> This will allow a direct connection between each individual and their family to the coverage, the cost, their care providers (of all kinds), and their legislator without regard to their status of employment. This direct connection will give us needed power, the users of the services, rather than to businesses and the government. A large business employee, a small business employee, an individual, a retiree, and a government-subsidized person, will all be under the same national health insurance program. All of us will pay an identical premium as someone else the same age, living in the same geography, and receiving the same government-mandated coverage from the same insurer.

5-9) Move all health care companies to nonprofit status.

This is the cornerstone requirement. Why?

National and individual health direction and decisions will no longer be driven by short-term profits and corresponding health care upper management paychecks. Instead, health care motivation will come from innovation. And innovation will come from the bottom up instead of the top down. Health care business leaders will now be supporting change innovators and long-term solutions to health issues instead of chasing the newest profit segment for business and personal gain. Even congressional lobbying will change to recommendations of long-term collaborative investment in innovative solutions to permanently solve chronic health issues rather than blocking regulation that may suppress profits. In addition to the current grant programs, under the nonprofit status, the federal government could provide a separate class of notes and bonds (coupled with significant underwriting, needs and success assessment, and audit controls) to encourage citizens to invest in more risky research of health issues like future antibiotics and dementia and many other significant issues.

The United States is one of the only countries in the world that does not regulate drug, medical device, and equipment company prices. Accordingly, the government must demand that all (even non-U.S. based) drug companies, medical device and equipment companies charge providers and us (on our behalf) no more than the lowest international price of the products they sell. Obviously, some of these items are passed through to our insurance companies. Insurers would still be free to negotiate lower prices for their U.S. insureds if desired (thus increasing their profit or even further lowering our cost). One of our government agencies must audit drug and medical device and equipment manufacturers sale prices to international buyers annually and provide that base price to all licensed insurers and certain providers like hospitals and doctors. The audit process could be administered by one of several agencies and could be subcontracted to private audit firms.

Our lack of meaningful regulation has been the profit provider for all worldwide drug companies and medical device and equipment company profits…a huge source of our (U.S.) high cost of medical care (17% of GDP vs. less than 10% of GDP in most cases). Profits of drug companies and medical device and equipment companies must now be spread to other countries. We are not dictating their prices, only that we, the U.S. customers, get the best prices possible as the largest customer in the world of their products. This same requirement would be universal for all (including foreign) suppliers of drugs and medical devices and equipment.

10) The seven categories of health care.

By breaking health care cost into categories, we can gather data and evaluate cost of smaller buckets…even breaking the smaller buckets into even smaller buckets. Innovation advances will be able to be shared easily, and pricing adjustments can be recognized and implemented quickly. Awards can be given to innovative individuals, groups, and organizations. Cooperation rather than competition will be the driver of innovation. Research priorities will be driven by need rather than solely profit. (Profits and/or reserves are still mandatory to cover all costs, including research.)

11-18) Health insurance pricing.

All pricing would now be fair to all of us.

By eliminating all of the extraneous issues around pricing, such as employer—large or small business, employment status—working or not, healthy or not, deductibles, co-pays, and lifetime maximums or not, we get to the remaining few considerations for health care pricing…a government-mandated plan, age, geography, and insurer. It's simple. Look it up by insurer, and that's your monthly premium. Some of us will be subsidized because of Medicare or Medicaid or other government programs. Families just add the premiums together, but other than that, we just pay the bill (or have our employer withhold it from our paycheck if they are set up to do that) and deduct the annual net premium payments on our taxes.

The pricing process must be consistent between insurers and be consistent for comparable data collection by government regulators. If not set up and enforced in this manner, the result will again be intentional cost-shifting between markets and age categories to gain additional government subsidies and/or higher than required pricing.

Pooling of health insurance risks is another important factor. Generally, age is the only consistent indicator of higher health care costs, until we are diagnosed with a significant health issue. And yet that is exactly when we need insurance…and frankly, the definition of insurance…all of us pay something regularly to receive a benefit when we are the victim of a health issue. But health insurers and providers continue to fight to exclude us from coverage through extensive and expensive lobbying efforts. The following outlines why pooling must go if we are ever going to fix health care.

Health insurers group us into what they call pools of insureds. Each pool of insureds has a calculated profit or loss associated with it. If a pool is losing money, everyone in the pool gets a price increase, some larger than others.

In general, most health insurers have several pools. The following are the largest type of pools:

- Self-insureds—usually large organizations with hundreds, sometimes thousands, of employees. These are big businesses, governments, school systems, etc.

- Small organizations—usually small businesses with two to a few hundred employees.

- Individuals—usually a family unit or an individual.

- Medicare—retirees.

- Medicaid—government subsidized individuals.

As you might expect, the largest groups get the best pricing. These large groups are called self-insured because they only pay their exact costs plus an administration fee to an insurer to manage the cost payment process. This is one of the lowest-priced health insurance plans because there is no profit added to the paid costs...just the processing fee. Medicare and Medicaid (government programs) operate similarly to self-insureds. However, these government programs are even more restrictive about cost payments. The governments, state and federal, pay the insurer as an administrator, only a government approved value for each service rendered.

All of these restrictions placed on insurers by large organizations limit profits of insurers except in two areas—small businesses and individuals. Accordingly, insurers have used these two groups (pools in insurance-speak) to drive their most profitable business—a problem for all of us that are not part of large organizations, and a problem, as you will see later, contributing to issues around the Affordable Care Act—ACA).

Prior to the Affordable Care Act and its elimination of preexisting conditions, pooling was used as an effective tool to limit insurer risk from sick individuals and small businesses employing a sick individual. Insurers refused to insure them. Those employers and individuals were passed to state-run high-risk insurance pools. If a state had such a pool (and many did not—if not, you went without insurance), you generally paid about a 20% additional premium for less coverage than you or your business had in the past simply because you were unlucky...you were sick or you employed a sick person (or sick family member of a covered employee). Additionally, this state high-risk insurance was partially paid for by healthy individuals and healthy small businesses...again...you...prior to being sick or employing a sick person.

Interestingly, the same two small pools funded a significant share of insurer profit. Why did the large pools skirt any responsibility for the sick? ERISA (federal law enacted in 1974) allowed large groups to escape state taxes to help pay for the state's high-risk pool program. They often had operations in other states and therefore should be "allowed to follow federal law not state laws"...the argument for the law. A large business loophole was achieved by lobbying Congress. Some states built their high-risk pool using funds that bypassed ERISA by not taxing the insurance premiums but by taxing the service provider. Some states used general fund tax revenue to fund their high-risk pool.

Additionally, sick individuals are often outside of the large company health insurance pool, ironically, because large employers have better benefits programs. Over time, due to sickness-related absences and/or the sickness itself, sick individuals are moved out of the large company health insurance pool (and work) because of employer-provided disability insurance, and the company now needs to hire a replacement to fill the position. The disability insurance benefit makes this process easier for the large employer than it otherwise might be. For a time, if they can afford it, the displaced employee will receive large company corporate COBRA (continuing government-mandated health benefits—up to eighteen months) generally reasonably priced due to the self-insured price benefit scheme discussed later. But soon they end up as an individual with preexisting conditions looking for insurance at much higher prices.

Large employers pay insurers to process provider services' actual cost (doctors, hospitals, drug companies, etc.) plus an administration fee. Large employer business helps insurers pay for their provider payment administrative process, but it does not allow much profit on this business because the employer itself assumes the risk of profit and loss…meaning there can be no real insurer pricing/profit benefit to large employer business…just cost containment. Since almost all large companies and organizations have been using this method (self-insurance) of handling their employee health insurance program for decades, it is not a money-losing proposition.

On the other side, pooling of small employers and individuals into their own separate pools allowed insurers to price health insurance products with profits to cover the associated health risks. Conversely, insurers priced out or flat out denied health insurance coverage to any small business or individual (or family) if there were any significant health issues.

To this day, insurers continue to use pooling groups of insureds to justify artificial insurance company losses and/or exclude groups of sick or questionable risk groups (like small businesses or individuals) from obtaining insurance or pricing them out of coverage…even when profits from other lines of business are good. The bottom line: pooling is a shell game (cost-shifting) used by insurers to justify industry-wide higher prices and/or greater government subsidies.

Pooling is the cause of the Affordable Care Act's rapidly rising insurance premiums for small businesses and individuals.

As a small business buyer of health insurance during the early days of the Affordable Care Act, I lived through its trial run. Initially, under the Affordable Care Act, some insurers discounted premiums for individuals and small businesses alike to buy business, even with Obamacare's no health care screening requirement (preexisting conditions). Prior to Obamacare, many of these new customers had to buy, if available, state-subsidized health care or go without, as discussed earlier. Also, as discussed earlier, large businesses fund their own insurance, so there was no cost difference for them. However, insurers soon realized many of these new customers had bad health history. Consequently, with no preexisting health history required, insurers began raising premiums rapidly on individuals and small employers across the board. Even healthy individuals and small businesses were hit with huge premium increases...all due to the effects of pooling. The elimination of health histories in the application process merged all individuals, healthy or not, into the individual health pool and merged all small businesses, healthy or not, into the small business pool. Because of pooling and no health histories, all individuals and small businesses are assumed to be high risk. Premiums for the individual and small business pools skyrocketed. Premiums on Obamacare (ACA) are now at sustainable levels for the insurers but not for the affected small businesses and individuals. Many small businesses and individuals go without insurance due to the much higher premiums. Insurers either planned this, or they turned a mistake into a windfall. Either way, Obamacare (ACA) has turned bad business into good for insurers.

Under Medicare, the revitalized Medicare Advantage program, as a result of the elimination of the Medicare Cost Plus program, is set to do the same as Obamacare over time.

It will eliminate the better coverage of a Med Supplement program for two reasons. Similar to Obamacare, insurers are currently buying business with significantly cheaper pricing schemes than Med Supplements. The new Medicare Advantage policies are cheaper than Med Supplement policies but have limiting conditions that Med Supplements do not have. Just like Obamacare, rates will go up, and limiting conditions will get worse. Also, once you start down the Medicare Advantage path, you can not go back to a Med Supplement. Secondly, individuals who need the better coverage Med Supplement insurance due to existing health issues at sign-up (65-year-olds) for Medicare will buy up to the Med Supplement coverage because of its lack of limiting conditions. Accordingly, the Med Supplement program will, in the long run, be left with the sickest individuals who, again, will raise prices rapidly on Med Supplements. As with Obamacare, eventually all Medicare recipients will pay more for their supplemental insurance. Some will be priced out of the market, and taxpayers will be asked to pay up…again. This time, the insurers know exactly what they are doing. It worked so well with Obamacare, why not try it again? Another case of cost-shifting for profit.

There is another side to this which supports the nationwide health insurer model: my recommended Large Health Insurer model. As an example, in 2019, the Medicare Advantage program was aggressively promoted in Minnesota by Blue Cross Blue Shield of Minnesota (BCBS-MN), whereas the Med Supplement program was marketed in Minnesota by United Healthcare (UHC) and AARP. Why? BCBS-MN operates in Minnesota alone; UHC operates virtually nationwide. Advantage programs (BCBS-MN) allow insurers to require participants to use specified clinics and hospitals and are allowed to charge higher deductibles and copays in exchange for lower premiums. Therefore, insureds leaving their local area could have a big problem if they get sick while away. Because of higher copays and deductibles, you may end up paying more cumulatively than if you had chosen a Med Supplement program. Med Supplement programs (UHC) have no requirement to use specified clinics and hospitals. You can use any Medicare doctor anyplace in the U.S. You're even covered outside of the U.S. Additionally, you pay much lower copays and/or deductibles with the Med Supplement program.

In summary: because BCBS-MN can't control its non-Minnesota costs, it pushes the Advantage program. Whereas UHC, the much larger insurer, with nationwide networks, can control costs everywhere, so it offers Med Supplements, the better product, but still makes good money. That's my case for eight to ten large insurers who must write coverage everywhere.

However, in the future, as it stands now, I also believe because UHC is a for-profit company, it will adopt the strategy of pushing the Advantage program, too, to increase its stockholder return. You should also note that BCBS-MN operates in Minnesota as a non-profit business, but it is still not large enough to steer people into its Med Supplement program, the better product, due to limited out-of-state cost control. It offers Med Supplements but does not promote them. Consequently, a BCBS-MN Medical Supplement program will create less profit to protect and fund its business over the long run than the Advantage program. As of late 2020, for Medicare sign-up for 2021, UHC/AARP is now promoting Medicare Advantage. My earlier prediction is coming true.

Other advantages to the recommended price change strategies:

A) Additional pricing savings should be realized under the new nonprofit business status of all health care companies (not just insurers). Net profit of 10% or more after-tax prior health care revenue should be a removed premium cost to us insureds.

B) The price corridor/write everywhere regulations should limit substantially cherry-picking and drought areas of coverage and further level the pricing playing field with lower limits for all regions.

C) Limiting drug, medical device, and medical equipment pricing to the lowest number offered to the rest of the world will reduce our national insurance premium cost by moving some of it back to foreign countries.

D) Making the national health insurance program all-inclusive (including Medicare and Medicaid) we get the combined purchasing power of all of us. There are no longer buckets of money able to be pushed around by insurers to claim they are losing money and need higher premiums to cover certain groups (pools) of insureds. We will all get an increase, or we will all get a decrease.

E) And it should be a decrease if all of these ideas are put in place. You can't leave Big Business an opening, or they will move the money around, claim hardship, and need more money. Meaning Obamacare (ACA) and other laws are not the problems, but we must be vigilant in our pursuit of fairer, reasonably priced health care for all, adjusting our laws to achieve our goal. On the other hand, Big Business is the only one who can control the rise in costs....not government, not laws, not the (unbridled) free market. It will manage its costs, find a way to pay the bills and keep the doors open if we require Big Health's new focus to be to change to our long-term health, not their short-term profit, by changing health care corporate status from "for profit" to "not for profit."

19) Elimination of ERISA inconsistencies with new law.

As stated earlier, if all of the recommended changes are adopted, ERISA will no longer apply because health insurance responsibility will now be on each of us, not employers.

20-21) Legal issues costing insureds, our government, and us taxpayers needless premium dollars.

Because health care costs are so daunting, up to 17% of GDP, bad actors must be held accountable for their contribution to its cost. Two major problems are front and center currently: childhood smoking and opioid addiction. Both are accentuated by greed, and thus should be paid for out of the profits from greed...and the individuals responsible should spend time in federal prison.